From
People Pleaser
TO
BOUNDARY
BADASS

From
People Pleaser

TO
BOUNDARY
BADASS

Taljana Genys

GRAMMAR
FACTORY
— EST. 2013 —

Published by Grammar Factory Publishing, an imprint of
MacMillan Company Limited.

Grammar Factory Publishing
MacMillan Company Limited
25 Telegram Mews, 39th Floor, Suite 3906
Toronto, Ontario, Canada
M5V 3Z1

www.grammarfactory.com

Genys, Tatjana
From People Pleaser to Boundary Badass

Paperback ISBN 978-1-998756-86-5
eBook ISBN 978-1-998756-87-2

1. SEL023000 SELF-HELP / Personal Growth / Self-Esteem.
2. BIO026000 BIOGRAPHY & AUTOBIOGRAPHY / Memoirs.
3. SEL031000 SELF-HELP / Personal Growth / General.

PRODUCTION CREDITS
Interior layout design by Setareh Ashrafologhalai
Book production and editorial services by
Grammar Factory Publishing

Grammar Factory's Carbon Neutral Publishing Commitment
Grammar Factory Publishing is proud to be neutralising the carbon
footprint of all printed copies of its authors' books printed by or
ordered directly through Grammar Factory or its affiliated companies
through the purchase of Gold Standard-Certified International Offsets.

Dedicated to the silent sufferers,
in the hope that you too will
find your voice through my pages.

To the villains in my book, thank you!
You made me who I am today.

And to Bob, my rock throughout this
journey. You truly are one of a kind.

CONTENTS

AUTHOR'S NOTE

Dear Reader,

Thank you for purchasing this book! To say it has taken me on a journey is an understatement. What I had to learn, often the hard way, was how my mental state affected every aspect of my life, and why healing (myself and others) has become such a catalyst for me these days. In this book you will find me raw and honest, analysing and accepting my mistakes and the role I played in all of them. I am not proud of the journey and frankly, for the longest time I didn't want to publish the book as a result of it. Nevertheless, I chose to do so because I hope it will help others—you in particular, since you are now reading this book—to not repeat the mistakes I made.

I want to call out that this book is not meant to hurt anybody, even though I learnt by working through some chapters with my family and friends that it still did. So, please know that this book in its current form didn't come without sacrifice. I also want to highlight the references I make towards my ex-husband and emphasise that for the first seven years of our eleven-year marriage, we were incredibly happy. And while this journey is about him, it really is not. I have made my fair share of mistakes, as he has, and I hope that at some point this can come to a resolution. I also want to highlight that this came at a time I was very unhappy—at the beginning, truly, of my development journey. I have had a lot of healing to do—still do—and while healing is an ongoing journey, this book is intended to launch you on yours.

Finally, to my son—should you ever read this book, please forgive me for the journey it has taken you on. This book should really be dedicated to you.

INTRODUCTION

BEFORE I TELL you how I overcame it, I should begin by telling you how bad it was.

I always felt this sense of wanting to do 'the right thing' for everyone. Be 'the bigger person', as they call it, and stand above it all.

Little did I know I was using it as an excuse—that while pleasing others, I was hurting myself, big time!

Like I said, for the longest time I put this down to what we 'must endure' while following a path of higher purpose. Funny, the stories we tell ourselves to justify our own belief systems.

The truth was, I was suffering, and had been for years. Neglecting my needs had become such second nature to me that I didn't even question it. Not even when it went beyond relationships, touching *every* facet of my life. It had become such a habit that I didn't know anything different.

'How did this become such a part of your life?' you may wonder.

I'm glad you asked. I would roam the streets anxiously, dreading a conversation I needed to have weeks from then, trying to justify to myself that it was okay to say 'No'. Because saying 'No' meant upsetting people, and upsetting people meant getting the silent treatment—at least it had to me, in the past. Even now, thirty-odd years later, I could feel that fear in my body.

'Why didn't you do anything about it?'

Another great question. And the fact is, *I did*. I went through numerous development courses, completed a trauma course with Dr Gabor Maté, studied coaching, became 'addicted' to learning about human psychology. But no matter how much more I was able to comprehend the causes underlying my state of mind, using that knowledge to change it was something else.

MARCH 2022
(THREE MONTHS INTO
THE JOURNEY)

WAS ACCUSED OF having an affair with my neighbour today, by his on-and-off, overprotective girlfriend. She sent me a flurry of nervous text messages telling me it was unacceptable for me to speak to him every day.

The thing is, *we don't*. We became friends after I moved into my flat just under a year ago, but that's it.

A few days prior to sending those messages, his girlfriend had showed up at my doorstep, shaking and anxious. Naively, I tried to comfort her. I felt bad that she'd had to go through whatever she was going through, and confirmed, there and then, that nothing was going on between us.

Today, when she showed up accusing me, you could almost feel the unhealthy energy she was giving off; she was positively vibrating with insecurity. I asked her if she had read our messages, because if she did, she would have seen that I was on *her* side—I had tried to offer him some perspective, since I had gone through something similar not too long ago. I told her we were nothing but neighbours, and always will be—but I also said that she can't tell me who I can or can't speak to.

Pretty badass of me, I know! When I journaled on it later that day though, the first thought that popped into my mind was: 'Did I do the right thing?'

Then, I stopped myself and thought:

'Right by *whom*?'

I changed my approach, and began to ask myself different kinds of questions.

'Did I say the things *I* wanted to say?' Tick.

'Did I speak *my* truth?' Double tick.

Seeing those affirmative answers on the page made me feel surprisingly good. It made me realise that maybe I *was* on the way to becoming a badass, and how much I liked it.

Now I just needed to learn to do this in person, and be able to do it on the spot.

The following day

As it turned out, I popped the champagne bottle too quickly: the 'badass' woke up feeling not so great the next day.

'Why am I not feeling good?' I wondered. I went through my checklist of potential contributing factors as I wandered around the house.

Then it hit me—I was sitting in discomfort. The situation with my neighbour was unresolved, uncomfortable, and a little too close to home for my liking. (Literally.)

I was used to doing what others wanted, so *this* was new. While knowing I had drawn a line made me feel proud at first, now it was playing on my mind and making me feel tight in my belly.

Someone was upset, and *I* was the cause of it. And I was never the cause of it—something I made very sure of—

because the other thing I learned early on is that making someone upset had consequences. *Consequences my body still remembered…*

How it all began

I should tell you how much I freaked out when the title of this book first came into my head. I was still feeling pretty high after finishing my first book just days before, so when those words, and the truth behind them, landed in my lap and stared back at me so glaringly, it was quite confronting. Especially since I instantly knew how steep this hill would be. Frankly, I was afraid.

I tried pushing back on it, resisting it; I tried to find a new topic I could write about. But here's the thing about understanding your dharma: whether I wanted to accept it or not, the storm was already headed my way. And it was coming in fast.

The problem is, I *hate* confrontation; always have. One could even say that I go to great lengths to avoid it.

So what that meant was, it was time to dust off my armour and buckle up!

When I spoke to my coach about it a few days later, she told me to reframe my mind around the following message: 'I am enjoying the growth I will be getting from this.'

It made me gag. I was definitely not there yet, but I was determined to give this a go. I resolved that every situation that was thrown at me would become an opportunity to practise. Because I also knew the *real* issue it was trying to prepare me for—one I had been dreading for a few weeks now.

Being able to picture *that woman*, a.k.a. my ex-husband's new wife as *my teacher*, per my coach's recommendation, took a while. But eventually, it helped me reframe my mind to stop the resentment I was feeling, which had built up over several months.

This situation was a lot more complicated, though. Slowly, but steadily, Nina had crossed A LOT of boundaries about my boy—and I let her. Now that was upsetting for two reasons: one) considering how positively we started our relationship, and two) how friendly my ex-husband and I had parted ways. Something I was incredibly proud of, up until then. Family issues—especially when children are involved—are harder to deal with and a lot more complex than closing a door on a neighbour or turning down a random request. My brain kept circling around the consequences of my actions, making the 'sacrifice' become an easy excuse.

'I am doing this for my child,' I would tell myself. *Bullshit*, I finally called it today. I'm pretty sure he wouldn't want me to suffer on *his* account.

That too was a pattern of mine.

By the way, if you are in a similar situation right now, I reckon that my son came off a lot better the way things turned out between my ex-husband and me. Maybe not at first, or during the first few months of our separation, but now he gets double the holidays, double the presents and double the love. I'm not saying it's better than having Mum and Dad together (as long as they're functioning), but it's also not all bad.

Scratch that "not all bad" part—frankly, in my opinion, he *won the bloody lottery*, at least in our household. Whether it will always stay that way is yet to be seen.

Okay, back to the present...

My mobile rang, displaying my friend's number.

'I will pick you up at eleven,' she told me. 'Mind if we stop by my boyfriend's house on the way?'

'Of course not,' I replied. I had yet to meet him.

'He can't see you there,' she continued. 'I'll drop you off at a café and pick you up thirty minutes later. That okay?'

''Course it is!' I replied, way too quickly.

I have got to stop doing that. Of course it's *not* okay, at least not without an explanation. Knowing her, I know there will be a good reason behind it, and I will find out soon enough. But for now, this is yet another great example of how quickly I just say 'Yes' in order to please people.

'NO'.

'N-O'.

Two letters. It's really not that hard, is it? It's not hard to say it to myself all the time—so *why not to others*??!

The letter

I had written a letter in which I set a firm boundary with Nina, the new wife. The letter to her outlined her role in my son's life, recognising the importance of it, while asking her not to overstep it after she called herself his parent at school. Easy… right? The letter came to me several weeks ago and I had avoided it ever since.

When I say 'it came to me', I mean that I channelled it. After it came through, I wrote it down on my laptop so I wouldn't forget it, and then went for a run. A very long run.

Today I finally sat down and wrote it out on a piece of paper. The letter, to me, was very confronting. I re-read it about twenty times, asked for guidance about forty, wondered if I should share it with people who I knew would tell me to reconsider. But there was a deeper knowing inside of me, telling me that keeping this letter would be far more uncomfortable, for far longer.

The only difference? It would be uncomfortable for *me*, and that was a feeling I knew how to handle. I knew it would upset Nina to read this letter. I was knowingly doing something that was going to upset someone. It was eating me alive.

Anxiety spread through my heart and across my body, followed by nausea and a very unpleasant feeling in my gut—and it wasn't even time to send that letter yet! For all I knew, it wouldn't even happen this week...

No. It *had* to happen this week. Otherwise, I would simply go mad.

This is what I mean about being a people pleaser, and the discomfort it takes to draw the clear lines that will take you out of that role.

I WAS up until 3 a.m. that night, tossing and turning in bed. The fear I was experiencing was excruciating. I reviewed all the iterations of the letter that I had created, and then got back to the original one. When I re-read it in the wee morning hours, I realised that *nothing* I was going to say was going to be as painful as what I was experiencing.

It showed me how uncomfortable it is for me to even claim what is rightfully mine—my place in my son's life. So this morning I woke up and *understood.* This was the path I needed to walk, the hill I needed to climb to unlearn what I learned. And *this* was the strength that it would require.

But I still felt petrified. Even with all the countries I'd lived in throughout my life (four), the many challenges I'd faced in the past, all the different roles I'd had to play over the years, standing up for myself felt like the hardest thing I'd ever done.

I sent the letter to two friends. Subconsciously, I probably picked them out by design. The first friend would support my decision, the other would caution against it.

I didn't hear from my first friend, but I did hear from the second. Like I surely knew, she warned me of the letter's consequences, and questioned whether it would lead to a resolution.

I knew she was right. I posed myself those same questions over and over the night before. The easier path would be to *not* do it, and just swallow my pain.

But then, another question emerged:

'Was her upset more important than mine?'

I TOLD my ex-husband about the letter, and received a message from him an hour later. Nina was refusing to take the letter, and said that there would be no further exchange between us until I acknowledged her as a parent.

Multiple things happened within me when I got this message. First, a wave of anger washed over me. 'What do I do now?' came second. *Validation* hit third.

That reply suddenly confirmed *why* I had to do this. And, strangely, somehow it made it easier. I understood that unless I addressed this *now*, this would continue to be an uphill battle. So far, so good.

Then came the next part: sending it to my ex.

Once I hit send, I nearly puked. The cat was out of the bag, and there was nothing I could do to stop it.

It didn't take long. I missed a call from her while I was on a work call, and that was followed by a message moments later, telling me that 'my resentment and misery had no place in her life and that I can write as many letters as I liked, she would never read a written word of mine.'

As much as I want to say it was easy to respond to a reply like this, it really wasn't. Deep down inside, I knew she was resisting my letter, because of its reality.

'Another letter won't be necessary. Everything that needs to be said is in this one. There are some hard truths in there, which

are difficult to accept, I get that. Closing your eyes to them won't make them go away.'

I hit send, plugged in my headphones, and went for a run by the beach. I hadn't been a runner until then, but the past few months had somehow made me become one.

My sim card started playing up just as I left the house, and disconnected halfway through my track. No running coach in my ear, no motivational music—I was 'connection-free' for seven beautiful kilometres.

TWENTY-FOUR HOURS passed by without a response. Not that I could expect one, of course, but here's why it's worth mentioning: I still didn't know if Nina knew the content of the letter. And that was an important bit—as would be the repercussions that followed.

Closing loops with my neighbour

I needed to set the record straight with my neighbour. We hadn't spoken ever since his girlfriend rocked up in front of my door. I drafted a text, telling him that I would give them space to work things out and stop chatting to him in the meantime.

That was all good, right?

Not really.

As I re-read my message, it didn't feel right. I like my neighbour, and we get on great, in a purely platonic kind of way. So why was I saying goodbye and making things awkward?

Because someone else would be upset by our friendship.

'But—is that *my* responsibility?'

Now *this* was a new thought for me. Before, I would have been very happy to oblige. It would have been awkward bumping into him in future, sure, but this was 'the right thing to do'—right?

But again: right for *who*? *Who* am I always protecting?

In this case, it was somebody I barely knew. I had bumped into his girlfriend twice before she barged into my house, when they were already massively on the rocks (something he confided in me early on). And yet *her* emotional state seemed much more important to me than the one *I* had been living with for thirty-seven years now.

I recognised how messed up this was, and how much work I had to do. And I also knew the message I needed to send instead:

I clarified how I saw our relationship (purely platonic), but also how much I loved hanging out and noted that, if our friendship was causing issues, I was happy to take a step back and allow them to work things out. Because the last thing I wanted to do was get in between two people in a relationship.

(In hindsight I understood I did just that.)

Healing childhood wounds

I started working with my coach in November of 2021 (by far one of my best investments of that year), and today she did a regression session with me that was full of surprises. We had planned it for the past few weeks, and yet somehow we always managed to get sidetracked.

But today, forty-five minutes into our sixty-minute call, the urge to heal my mother wound came through stronger and stronger.

I should note here that my mother and I have been on a journey of deepening our relationship ever since I started writing this book. Back then, a lot of things were still unresolved—today, I count her as one of the people I confide in, which has been pretty significant for me. For that alone I am grateful for this book.

Now back to the call. I understood I had to ask for the regression session to still take place and, looking at the time, the likelihood was growing smaller and smaller by the minute. When I finally did, my coach agreed to still go ahead with it. And it was incredibly profound.

She guided me through a visualisation in which I found my mother sitting on a bench. She must have been nineteen, maybe twenty years old, and we ended up working through my mum's wound, not mine. Since I am in no position to speak to the wounds of others, I will leave it there, but what is worth noting is that I learned about intergenerational karma that day—which meant that if I didn't deal with it now, it would transfer onto my son as well at some stage. Now that wasn't something I was just going to accept in any form (I think any mother can relate). So I accepted my 'mission' to heal our ancestors' karma and all it required me to do.

The fascinating part was, I started crying the second I walked through the portal my coach guided me through ... the body knows.

I then asked all my ancestors to walk this path beside me, to support and guide me in moments I felt lost, and especially in moments I stopped believing in myself. Because accepting this didn't mean I wasn't afraid. I just couldn't let my fear stop me any longer. And my son was a pretty good incentive for that.

(In hindsight, that moment probably showed me what my mother needed from me).

Healing the *actual* childhood wound

The session with my coach taught me I needed to take Mum on this journey with me. I called her, and we agreed to speak fifteen minutes after my call.

I should clarify: At that time, my mother and I didn't speak very often. Absorbed in my own healing process, I had distanced myself from her following my divorce. How much should I tell her?

It would probably be best to start at the beginning—but where was that? When the idea for this book first came through? Or in my childhood, where it all began?

The feeling in my body was quite interesting: I was nervous and emotional at the same time. It was similar to how I felt before the regression session with my coach.

Why was I nervous?

Because I knew deep down inside that I needed to tell my mum that this journey was about where it had originated from—my childhood—and how that made me who I am today. That among all the beautiful moments we shared in the past, there were several moments that impacted me deeply.

We spoke for an hour and fifty-six minutes—the longest conversation we had had on the phone since my move.

I spoke for ninety per cent of the time (also a first, back then).

In the past, I realised at that moment, I had leaned more often on my father, creating a bigger gap between my mother and me.

It wasn't easy in the beginning, but then it all just came out somehow. One after the other, I told her about the book, Nina, the regression session, what I learnt about ancestral healing, my dharma. Lastly, I brought up my childhood.

It all happened kind of quickly, and I was glad it did. It gave us a chance to reconnect at a deeper level, in our truth. I've always craved a closer connection with my mother, and today I realised it took both of us to get there. I realised in that moment, that I hadn't let her in lately either—not properly, at least. A key ingredient for a deeper connection, and to someone seeking to establish a stronger bond.

The other thing today showed was that blood truly is thicker than water. Your family *will* be there for you, if you just ask.

A few hours later, my dad left me the most beautiful voicemail on their behalf, expressing his and Mum`s support for my book and taking responsibility for the part they played in it. They gave me permission to put everything I needed into the pages of this book, and said that both of them take accountability for their mistakes

Needless to say, I was crying as I was writing this, just as I was when I received that message. Because *this* is what unconditional support of someone's purpose truly looks like.

MY PARENTS were very young when they had my sister and me, and while I blamed them for many things in the past, having my own child at the age of twenty-five gave me perspective—especially after I learned how we do what we do based on how we were brought up. They too did what they knew, until they knew better.

Like them, I also made a lot of mistakes with my own son, especially during his first few years, and would do many things differently now if I could turn back time. Starting with talking to him about boundaries. *Today*. (Minus the context of what got me to this point, obviously; he doesn't need to know what's happening between his stepmother and me at that stage.)

In our conversation about boundaries, I told him to listen to his body, and to speak up when something feels off—including when it was happening with me. I gave him the example of when I overstepped a boundary with him in the past, when we had gone to the Gold Coast for the first time with a plan to visit every theme park there was. I had convinced him to go on a rollercoaster ride he was petrified of. At the time, I thought I was doing him a favour, that he'd love it if he tried it. I couldn't have been more wrong. He started crying the second the seat belt was fastened, and still doesn't *ever* want to go on a rollercoaster again.

If I could turn back time and change my actions, this would be the moment I would probably start with. The other would be when I tried getting him into the sea for his swimming lessons, with pretty much the same result. We live and learn.

I am sharing these stories with you to illustrate how, even though some signs are very visible, we still ignore them because we worry too much about what *others* will think, instead of listening to what is going on for *them*. These are the moments we teach our children to ignore their emotions, and this is where people-pleasing is born (as well as so many other kinds of trauma).

So, for whatever 'wrong' my parents did in the past, they also did a lot right. Especially in the moments that mattered the most.

A cinema visit with a kick

My son and I decided to go to the movies today. At the cinema, he asked if he could call his dad to check which movie they were going to see the next time they were together before we chose ours. I was surprised, and a little taken aback, but it only hit me when I got home: he might be developing his own people-pleasing skills as we speak. Which made it all the more important that I learn how to fix mine, in order to teach him how to fix his.

His dad asked where we were, and I panicked. This simple question put me into overdrive. I imagined him and Nina showing up at the movies, confronting us outside and wanting to talk about the letter. It was silly to think that way, of course, since it was merely an innocent question. But I am sharing this with you to illustrate how big the issue of the letter had become in my head. After all, our minds determine our wellbeing.

For all I knew, my ex could have deleted the message that contained the letter to Nina. But rational thinking didn't help me where I was right then; still sitting deep in discomfort and the unknown.

I WAS tossing and turning in bed again that night until something quite peculiar happened: I got *fed up*. Fed up with the situation, and fed up with feeling weak.

The strong side of my character was starting to emerge. *Enough was enough!*

My coach's words were ringing in my ears: 'How much longer do you want to suffer?'

I didn't. Not any more.

Needless to say, I didn't get a lot of sleep that night, but it didn't matter.

THE NEXT morning, I got my son ready for school and then went for a run. The route was labelled the 'Be True' run on the Nike running app. Five kilometres of remembering who I was. (I highly recommend you try it out.)

As I was passing a sports field, I found a big puddle in front of me. One so big I had to go around it.

That's when it clicked. *That's* what I had to do with the challenge at hand—I had to go around it, instead of marching right through it like I was doing right now. But how?

Birthday shenanigans

It was the last week of March, which also happens to be my birthday week, and I was *so* excited! New year, new life, new me, here I come! I was *so* ready for it.

I have always liked birthdays and new years for their potential, and for the first time in years, I made a lot of plans to celebrate this one big. Because I was learning to love myself, which also meant I was ready to be loved by others.

One of those plans included a celebratory lunch with a friend. As I was about to leave the house, we debated if she should come get me or if I should take the bus for far longer than necessary.

Suddenly, it hit me: I was making the whole thing unnecessarily complicated, because the people pleaser in me didn't want to inconvenience anyone. *Not even on my birthday.*

Once I understood that, I surrendered: I said 'Yes please!' to being picked up, and to all the other wonderful surprises she had in store for me that day.

It became the year I truly received all my birthday wishes and blessings, and actually let people celebrate me in a whole new way.

It was also the week I was going to sit in my first Ayahuasca ceremony.

I always knew this would become part of my journey at some point, but never knew the profound effect it would have on my life—and this journey in particular.

I also knew not to go looking for it, that when the time was right, the medicine would come find me. And 'she' did—two months into this journey, the only other time I sat with another plant.

Now, this isn't usually something I share very openly, and I should pre-empt here that I have the highest respect for *safely administered* plant medicine to aid a healing process, don't use it recreationally, and consider it a sacred healing modality. While I had experimented with other substances in the past, this was no longer part of my present. This was something I made very sure of by avoiding the majority of drink-fuelled events. So when it occurred to me to include it in the book, I panicked—big time. Telling people about it was never part of the plan, especially when I didn't know where they stood on the subject.

But I do feel called to mention it for two reasons: one) to reinforce its importance, and two) to advise anybody going on that journey to do so in a safe manner. It is a plant I have learned to respect in many ways over the years—based on the guidance I received from it, and the illusions that it showed me.

But more on that later.

At first, I thought it was just fear of judgement, but then I realised it was something else. This was another form of people-pleasing. Selective sharing might be a good form of self-protection, but if I wanted to live my truest, most authentic life, I needed to learn to be okay with people not approving of my choices. Hear opinions I did not want to hear, accept that I won't be everybody's cup of tea, and be okay with that.

Now, that's a lot easier said than done, especially for a recovering people pleaser. No one likes criticism, and I am no exception.

But then I realised something else. Maybe more important than being liked by many, is that I be liked by one—myself. For the life I was living, and the choices I was making.

After all, one life is all we get.

I thought back to one of the speakers I listened to a while back, talking about 'life without regrets', and remembered nodding along agreeably as he spoke. But how often did I actually live that way? And if I lived truly unapologetically, the way I thought was right, did it even matter what others thought?

Well, sure—sometimes. But more important is that, while opinions will come and go, my life, my worth and my independence will stay with me forever.

So, while this might not have been where I planned to take this journey, what's a ride without a rodeo?

April

I went to a sacred dance party today, a birthday gift I had given to myself, accompanied by two of my girlfriends. The idea was to reconnect with our bodies in a circle of about twelve women, dancing to seven stages of rhythm in dim lighting, booze-free.

I hadn't been out in ages, so, giddy with excitement, wearing a little red jumpsuit and my friend's red lipstick, I sat down beside the other women to listen to the instructor talk us through the seven stages. The first three songs were the warm-up, followed by the fun stage, the sexy stage, the purge, the release, the heart-space stage and the remembering stage.

As the instructor was describing the different stages, I already started judging them. This wasn't what I had imagined for my birthday celebration. Dancing? *Yes*! Fun? *Yes*! Being told *how to* dance and *when*? *Nooooooo*.

Sexy dancing on cue? *HELL no*.

Those feelings persisted on the dance floor, especially once the sexy stage kicked in. I was moving my body around awkwardly, judging my level of sexiness left, right and centre. Until suddenly, I stopped. A question came into my head.

Who was I trying to be sexy *for*?

As soon as that insight hit, I surrendered.

Let go.

Broke free.

And had the *best freaking time*!

I danced, I hoped, I screamed, I went down on the floor and let my body take over as I surrendered to the music. At the purge stage (the fastest part of the night), my whole body started to shake violently, purposefully and aggressively. The more I shook, the more I could feel something being kicked out of me—*the people pleaser*.

It was being evacuated from my body by something stronger that was being born within me, something that was coming to fill its place—*the badass*.

It's hard to describe what truly happened to me that night, but it was insanely liberating.

My head jumped back in at the 'remembering stage', when we were meant to be in meditation, and told me off when my thoughts trailed off for just one moment. Then those same thoughts suddenly started fighting back. I could hear myself put judgement back in its place, tell it that I had had enough of being told what I *could* or *couldn't* do, *think* or *couldn't think*, and that whoever's judgement that *was,* and *wherever it came from*, that it wasn't needed anymore. And then I found myself thanking it for times it helped me in the past, before wishing it farewell.

And with that, a new me was born—right there and then in a little warehouse out in Brookvale, next to eleven other women on the dance floor, each on their own path of re-discovery.

Meeting resistance

A few days later I was supposed to catch up with Lauren, who I had met at a recent women's retreat. Yet right from when I woke up that morning, I felt like I didn't want to meet her.

'Why?' I asked myself.

Lauren was in a difficult stage in her life, and had shown interest in plant medicine after going through severe depression. The woman who introduced me to the medicine had volunteered my name to her, without checking with me first.

So, there were two plausible reasons for my hesitation:

1 I didn't want to be in her energy, or

2 I wasn't ready to open myself up to sharing my plant medicine journey openly.

(In hindsight it ended up being the latter.)

I journaled on it before leaving the house, my resistance still rising, and pulled an oracle card for direction. A second card jumped out at me, after I had already pulled my first. It read 'See your inner beauty.'

This card had been my frequent companion lately: I had already pulled it before the sacred dance the other day, and then again before my birthday night out. It also happened to be the cover of the oracle deck.

Today, it told me it was time to look within. With that thought in mind, I met Lauren outside my house. I suggested she leave her car on a side street so we could go for a walk and not worry about parking. She agreed, and we set off.

To my surprise, the meet-up turned out to be a very pleasant day and an easy walk. After about twenty minutes of light-hearted conversation, I finally opened up to Lauren about my first experience sitting with the other plant.

Lauren listened intently, asked a question here or there, and made me feel very comfortable. Right up until we got back to her car, and she found a parking ticket on her windscreen. Everything changed in that moment.

'You told me I could park here,' she said, anger coming through in her voice.

I felt horrible. It was as if everything that happened up until then had gone with the wind. She drove off.

I went inside the house, debating where to go from here for a moment. Part of me wanted to apologise, the other pay for her ticket—or half of it, at the very least. Then I stopped myself and recalled the whole scenario.

Yes, I had told her she could park on that street, and should have double-checked when I left the house, out of courtesy. Maybe I would have seen her car parked on a yellow line, which had not been visible to me from where I was coming to meet her. But this wasn't *my fault*.

So, I sent her the following message:

> *'I feel bad about your ticket. I should have checked where you parked before we left. I know finances are tight at the moment, let me know if I can help.'*

She replied two hours later, telling me she had written to the council to dispute the ticket, and that she had had a wonderful time and was grateful for all the insights I had given her.

The people pleaser in me wanted to ask, 'You sure?' But again, I stopped myself. Instead, I told her I was glad we had met, and thanked her for coming on the journey with me.

Turns out you *can* teach an old dog new tricks.

Preparing for what was to come

The weekend ceremony I had booked for my birthday required me to cut out caffeine, sugar, salt and most spices for five to seven days prior to the sitting, as well as other pleasures I currently wasn't enjoying in life. It was designed to ensure that you're the cleanest possible channel to work with the medicine, and to help you to centre within yourself and the intention you set for the 'retreat'.

Needless to say, life got pretty bland for a while—especially for a foodie and coffeeholic like me. My mood plummeted, and so did the weather. It was raining so hard that we eventually got another message from the organiser informing us that the event would be confirmed or cancelled by Thursday, since the increased water levels limited access to the grounds.

This was heartbreaking news to receive a second time round, given that my first weekend had already been rescheduled to this one. I wasn't sure I had it in me to potentially face that for a third time.

In the meantime, the deadline for my first book was fast approaching. I had yet to edit the last hundred and fifty pages before submitting, and it was feeling harder and harder by the minute.

The call with my coach that morning saved me. It turned out that I was grieving the completion of my first book, and was afraid of where it would take me from here. It was similar to when you're leaving primary school to start high school, my coach explained: it's daunting.

This wasn't something I was conscious of, and it's another reason why I highly recommend working with a coach. That insight literally changed everything within seconds: she helped me reframe my situation and look at my final pages as 'tying the bow to a gift'. I had already bought the gift, and wrapped the gift—all that was left was to tie the bow. With this new outlook, I got to work and finished re-editing the book just after midnight—a feat that I had thought was impossible barely eleven hours before.

When the confirmation for the retreat came through just twelve hours later, I was both excited and ready to puke. It suddenly became very, *very* real.

As you might guess, I didn't sleep much that night. Lying awake, I listened to other people's experiences via podcasts and other media platforms. It's probably not something I would recommend before the first sitting: while it gave good insights about what to do before and after the ceremony, as well as mantras to use in case it got hard, I also learned about some experiences that I could happily have gone without hearing the night before I faced the ceremony myself.

With that thought in mind, I set off the following morning.

The journey

I can imagine that all this wasn't what you expected to read when you first picked up this book, but I ask you to bear with me until the end. Because this was also not the story I had intended to write at the time the title came through.

I could have easily left this section out, kept it to myself and merely focused on my experiences, but you will hopefully soon understand why I chose not to—because, as you'll see, of how much I changed as a result.

Could I have become the same person without the medicine? Potentially.

Could I have done it in the same amount of time? Not a chance.

I arrived for the first ceremony in the early afternoon. My head had been hurting all day, as the hours in front of my laptop and the lack of sleep from the night before were catching up with me quickly. Not to mention the fasting since lunchtime.

Reviewing my intentions in my head, I bounced back and forth between surrendering to the medicine and asking to see truth in everything. Outside my intentions, I had also added a healthy list of asks—for good measure, you know?

I asked for help to mend my relationship with Nina, and to become stronger in myself. I asked to better align with my purpose and to stop beating myself up all the time.

Tired and overloaded, I started preparing for the five-hour journey ahead, when the argument with my ex-husband on the way here popped back to mind.

A significant chunk of money had disappeared from my son's savings account in one transaction—money, I later learned, that was invested in crypto currency, and money he had received from my mum and dad. In hindsight, maybe not such a big deal, but what I felt needed to be called out in that moment was that a withdrawal of that size warranted a conversation ahead of time—even if the money was put to good use (as in this case). And yet, as I sat there waiting for the ceremony to start, I once again started questioning if I was right or wrong, and if I was acting out of ego.

It boiled down to my biggest challenge: I never knew when I was right anymore, unless I pleased. It was programmed within me so deeply that only other people's perceptions were able to determine what was right or wrong for me.

This was why I needed some *healthy* external validation on hand as I set out on this unknown path—whether it came through my coach, or the friend who joined me on this journey. I needed to know when I was on the right track, and when it was time to unlearn what I thought I knew in the past.

With that in mind, I entered the maloca at eight o'clock that evening, where I found both death and salvation in just one sitting.

THE ROOM was filled with ten mattresses. The one I had randomly chosen happened to be right next to where the shaman would sit.

Feathers, buckets, toilet paper and a big gong were spread out across the room. It was hot, a little fire oven keeping the maloca toasty.

'The journey will begin in fifteen minutes,' we were told by one of the shaman's assistants.

My headache didn't subside, but something told me this was going to be part of the experience. As I looked around the room, there was a calm within me I didn't recognise, especially after the podcasts I had listened to the night before.

I was ready—for whatever was in store for me that day.

We were a group of ten individuals, and a few of us were experiencing it for the first time. That gave me great comfort, as did knowing that this wasn't the first rodeo for some of the others. But more importantly, I felt super-connected to the energy of the shaman, and trusted in the healing powers of the plant.

The liquid, the shaman had explained to us earlier, was a combination of a leaf, a vine and tobacco. He had been taught how to brew it by a tribe in Ecuador, and explained that it was the precise combination of the three that made the medicine so effective.

He entered the maloca and started cleansing himself, then us, with tobacco, agua de Florida, and some ingredients I didn't recognise. Later, he called in the directions before opening the space and calling us forward to receive our first brew.

One by one, we came up to him and breathed our intention into the cup, before sculling the liquid down as quickly as possible. The effects would set in about thirty minutes later.

When it was my time to set my intention, I suddenly felt an urge to repeat the following mantra:

'I surrender to the will of the universe.'

I kept saying it over and over again, quietly and with deep conviction. And then, after I closed my eyes for a mere moment, a big snake appeared right in front of me—just before I had my first sip of medicine.

'Help me remember,' I heard myself whisper. The snake nodded and disappeared.

The snake is the symbol of Ayahuasca, and it later also turned out to be my totem animal. But in that moment, it just told me I was safe. That there was a reason I was in this room with all the others, and whatever that was, it was going to be okay.

Just then, the shaman called my name and offered me my first cup.

THERE WERE three opportunities to drink the medicine throughout the night. The rule of thumb was, if you could make it to the altar, you were good to have more of the brew. The second rule was to try to keep it down for as long as possible, so it had a chance to enter your body and activate the healing.

When the shaman asked how I wanted to start the journey—light, medium or strong—I panicked. How do you decide on the right dose for a medicine you've never had? Was this the moment to be courageous, or sensible?

'I don't know', I whispered, honestly.

He poured my drink intuitively, added the tobacco, whispered something into my cup, and handed me my drink.

'Help me remember,' I said again, quietly, and held the cup to my heart.

'Salute,' I then called out, and downed the liquid.

It wasn't as vile as I imagined—though it turns out that the taste gets worse the more you drink it. Once everybody had had their cup, the shaman wished us a good night and dimmed the lights. There we were, ten strangers sitting in total darkness, waiting for our journeys to begin.

I lost all concept of time for a while, until someone started vomiting a few seats away from me, snapping me back into reality. I tried holding onto the liquid even more from then on.

Then something unexpected happened: I started to feel good. *Real* good.

No one had mentioned feeling good in any of this, so this took me by surprise. Actually, I didn't just start to feel good, I felt GREAT! Colours started appearing in front of me as shapes came forward to upgrade my frequency, so I could start doing the inner work.

It didn't last very long. The effects wore off again quickly, and a message came through my mind telling me to ask for a stronger drink.

I made my way back to the shaman as soon as he offered. This time, I set the intention for the medicine to 'hit me'.

And it did. I barely made it back to the mattress before it all began.

First, I lost all control over my body and mind. As I released my 'healing' into the bucket, I was shown what I was holding onto, my body moving back and forth violently, showing me memories of the past.

The surprising part was that it wasn't disgusting, even though I puked nearly half of the night. Not even the snot running from my nose bothered me that evening. It all somehow became part of the experience, teaching me to love myself no matter what. While I was being cheered on by my ancestors for doing the work, colour and love surrounded me.

The noises that left my mouth that night were terrifying, and yet the experience wasn't. Even the sounds of others releasing sounded healing somehow.

I didn't let go of my bucket for most of the night, even though my body was swaying around dangerously as I shook off the expectations that were put upon me to 'have to be' a certain way. I was literally stripping it off my body.

Pain, loneliness, hurt and regret hit me next, a wave of sadness leaving my body as one of the shaman songs reminded me of my last relationship. I cried big tears deep from my heart, realising only then how much sadness I was holding inside.

Then, Nina came through.

'Sister,' I heard myself calling out to her, remembering our soul contract, connecting with her on the one thing we had in common: 'our' one and only, my son. I was grieving not having a second baby, while she wished to be a mother. With that, my son became what connected us, and also what drove us apart. He was our only opportunity to experience it all, and both of us wanted to make the most of it.

A message came through for her later that night, one that I would send her a few days later.

The rest of the night was spent healing my back pain and its origin, connecting me back to my roots, and sitting with the others in love and gratitude, before the third cup released my karmic linkage.

I barely made it to the shaman for my last cup. I sat in front of him humbly, and in total awe of the work he was doing and the light he was shining. Light I was able to see as I drank my third cup.

When we closed out the ceremony, I was in absolute gratitude that the medicine had found me, and for everything it brought.

WE FASTED until midday the following morning. This time, I didn't mind. I was still in a bubble of bliss as I walked the land barefoot, though my throat was hurting from the night of release.

Over lunch, we exchanged our experiences with each other while chewing on root vegetables. The dynamic had noticeably shifted. No longer were we ten strangers; it felt more like we were brothers and sisters who had met on the other side.

We cleaned our buckets and released our 'healing' back into nature, before the shaman sprinkled ashes over them and cemented the procedure with mapacho.

Ready and excited to do it all again, I stepped back inside the maloca just hours later.

THE SECOND journey couldn't have been more different from the first. It took me days to move on from it, and another week to stop calling it a total disaster.

I had stepped up to the altar like the night before, asking for a strong journey from the start, and felt the effect moving through my body almost instantly. But my connection broke seconds later, all colours and lights disappeared, and my journey became not individual, but *very* present to it all. Especially to the vomiting going on all around me.

I told the shaman I was unable to connect when he handed me my second cup, and he filled it with more medicine. But even then, nothing.

When I finally managed to purge that night, it was a real struggle. Gone were the cheering, the lights and the insights. The shaman came over and began to sing to me, tapping my back with branches of the vine. He covered me in tobacco and whispered something in my ear.

That was all it took. I started vomiting violently like never before. But, unlike yesterday, the smell was vile—so vile, I couldn't bear to be anywhere *near* my bucket.

I felt cold and alone that night, and was unable to shake it off long after the ceremony. Not even when I stepped outside and sat by the fire, or when I begged and prayed for support, or when I cried wholeheartedly. As much as I tried, I was unable to surrender and accept the process for what it was. I literally begged the third cup for relief, but it brought nothing but more darkness.

When the ceremony finally came to a close, my friend came over and hugged me. I started to cry into her embrace, realising how much I had longed for that hug all night. Afraid and alone, that night was my return to innocence. Like a baby, I had landed back on Earth, cold and afraid. Nothing could soothe me apart from love and affection, my shadow teaching me to look after myself more.

While I had craved to connect with the medicine, it had instead forced me to connect to my darkness—so that I could know and learn from it, and later channel it to heal the darkness of others. It was an old shamanic belief, I was told, and something it took me days to fully comprehend.

That night was my rebirth. Stripped of all I knew, confused and lost, it was the end, but also the beginning. I didn't *love* the experience the second night, didn't love my bucket, and didn't love releasing it all. And yet I learned to appreciate the duality of life, and that light has to face darkness so that we can appreciate light even more.

The journey after the journey

Walking the streets in the following days felt like a big release. I felt the change instantly. No longer was I looking at others for validation or feeling the need to smile at everyone who passed: I just walked and allowed myself to *be*.

Was this how others felt all the time? It was liberating.

At breakfast I wasn't anxious when my son went silent, but understood he was just in his own head. What a difference from how I would have felt just a week ago! That's when I finally had the courage to send Nina the message that came through when I was in the ceremony:

> *'I sat in ceremony this weekend to heal and mend our relationship. I accept you are playing a parental role in my son's life. My ask is you respect mine as his biological mother. Only when both statements are true, can true healing occur.*
>
> *I will wait for you to come find me.'*

I HAD a lot of dreams again that following night, my body and brain seemingly still catching up with the experience.

In the morning, I thought about the session I had with the spiritual accelerator group the night before. My soul tribe. Last night's topic:

Psychic readings through oracle cards

We were asked to pick an area in our life we wanted guidance on, and I couldn't decide. Where did I need direction the most? My purpose?

Nina came to mind. I hadn't heard from her since my message, and took that as a good sign. Topics like these usually required some thought.

We were guided into our meditation, and the woman I was paired up with beamed from ear to ear.

'I am so excited to do your reading today,' she said, laying out three cards in front of me.

The card highlighting my past revealed what the ceremony had already shown me: that Nina and I were indeed, connected through a past life. That this wasn't our first rodeo together.

'What is my next step?' I asked. 'Will Nina be as willing to try to work this out as I am?'

Instead of an answer, I received another question:

'Are you still seeking her love and approval?'

I thought about it for a moment. *Respect* is what I had asked her for, but yes—on a deeper level, I guess I was.

'Don't', came the reply, firmly. 'Let it go and focus on you. You will need to make a decision about your path very soon.'

WHEN I woke up the following morning, I found myself wanting to call my parents and tell them about my recent experience sitting with the plant.

Now *this* was unusual for me. As I mentioned before, at that time I didn't tend to share a lot with my family, especially when it came to topics like these. And yet for some reason I wanted to take them on the journey with me this time, and explain to them at length what I had just experienced.

All masks fell from me as I spoke my truth that day. A new sense of authenticity infused me as I shared my views openly like never before.

My parents were understandably curious about my experience, and questioned what this meant, naturally concerned about where this path could potentially take me. But over time, they would be able to see for themselves the profound impact this work had had on my life. Energy doesn't lie, and neither does a healthy heart. Let the work do the talking.

For now, though, I realised that not everybody would be on board with my new path, and that, sooner or later, going on this journey would mean losing people along the way.

'As long as I don't lose myself again,' came my reply.

Choosing your purpose

The following day, I realised that I had set myself an impossible goal.

I was waiting for my purpose to find me—when it couldn't find me, I had to *choose* it!

That realisation hit me moments after I hung up the phone with my parents. It was triggered by a dream I'd had for two consecutive nights of my next shamanic teacher (or her energy, I should clarify), after asking for guidance about it just a few days before. When I finally told my parents about the weekend I'd just had, *her face came through*, midway through our conversation.

It was then it finally clicked why I had to tell them. *Needed* to tell them.

This is who I *was*, and I needed them to see me for *me*.

I had always felt something shamanic inside me, and yet for one reason or another I kept waiting for someone else to see it too. Maybe I never *truly* believed it, right up until that moment.

I messaged the shaman I had dreamed of that same afternoon. Since I didn't have her number, I slid into her DMs, explained what had just happened, and asked if it was possible for us to connect. Universe, over to you!

Ruby, the shaman, replied a few days later. I had met Ruby in Bali just over five years ago, in the middle of my separation from my ex-husband. We barely exchanged five sentences at the time. I should add how peculiar it is that she is the person I am connecting with, and how I would never have guessed it in a million years.

After I texted her, she explained that she connects people between the upper and lower world, and asked what I was looking for specifically.

Therein lay the whole challenge—I had no idea! All I could do was follow the breadcrumbs.

So I told her just that. At the risk of sounding like a complete lunatic, I told her about her energy coming through to me two nights in a row; about my Native American spirit guides and animal spirit team; and how the ceremony had led me to commit to my spiritual path more than ever.

While I was messaging with Ruby, I was waiting for my ex-husband to pick up our son—and with him, the gift and card that included the letter. The closer it came to pick-up time, the more anxious I got.

'You've done your part,' my brain tried justifying to me. My intestines weren't so convinced, however.

'You need to honour yourself,' my brain tried again. 'You don't need their love and approval.'

Again, easier said than done. Turns out old habits truly do die hard.

But I realised *what* I was afraid of had changed. I wasn't afraid of handing over the letter any more, or how it would land. That part felt right. More than right actually: it was the gateway to respect, the start of understanding, and the beginning of any possible hope of reconciliation.

No—I was afraid they wouldn't take the letter. Healing cannot occur as long as eyes and ears aren't open.

So when my son left with the bag, I waited for a few more minutes. That's when the calm finally set in.

The ball was rolling. And as much chance as there was that the letter would land in the bin as soon as they got home, there was also the smallest chance it would finally reach its destination. Later I understood I had also crossed her boundary—big time. And that wasn't a good approach. While I still firmly believe this boundary needed to be set, I wish I had considered a more gentle approach. So for anybody reading these pages, know that boundaries can be set with a sledgehammer, or with a more sensible approach. I highly recommend you opt for the latter.

I RAN twenty-one kilometres the following day, my prep run for the half marathon. I still couldn't believe my friend had talked me into it—or that I was actually running, for that matter. I guess anyone can become a runner when life becomes hard enough.

It was meant to be 'only' eighteen kilometres that day, but I got lost halfway through the run after being redirected by a red-bellied black snake. Welcome to Australia!

It was a hard run that morning, and not just because of the snake. The terrain was rocky, the roads flooded and the only way through was through, for the most part. At one point, I landed on my knees after a stumble, and then fell face down to the ground. Luckily, my phone caught the bulk of it.

That was at the eleven-kilometre mark, and there was no way of turning back. Instead, I thought about the dream I had had the night before, which was about finishing the run this morning. So, I pushed on.

My ex-husband and his wife were part of that dream too, as was my healing modality.

When I woke up, I found a message from Ruby on my phone, confirming our call for the following Tuesday.

My stomach did a somersault. I still had no idea what I was going to tell her, or what I should ask for at that stage. Part of me was hoping I would get some clarity on that this morning.

Instead, I was reminded of my vows to my ex-husband, asked to reach out to the man I was currently in love with, and got to revisit moments I shared with my family and friends over the years.

The universe works in mysterious ways...

MY THOUGHTS were all over the place the following morning. In my scattered state, I felt an urge to sit by the sea. Water has always had a strong grounding effect on me, even more so on a day like today, after the full moon.

I sat by the ocean and journaled, question after question tumbling out onto the paper. I didn't get any insights on Peru that night (an ask I had set out the evening before).

Quite randomly, I was told to go to Peru many years ago by a tarot reader I met in Bali, who read me my fortune out of the blue. Back then, I ignored the request. I had just returned from yet another work trip overseas, had already taken time out for the development course I was there for, and, with my son still being little, the timing just felt completely off.

I should have known that once those doors close, they don't reopen very quickly. It's been six years, and I've been trying to get back on that path ever since.

Was I asking the wrong questions?

My past-life regression session popped into my mind. I had done a short version not long ago with the spiritual accelerator group, with mixed results. Yet it showed up again during my integration session a few days earlier.

Dark clouds were leaving my body as the darkness I sat with during the second night of the ceremony evaporated. As it did, my body shared some insights with me from a past life as a shaman—one that didn't end very well, I should add, as it also came with a warning to watch out for bad spirits surrounding me. One man in particular was highlighted to me—someone I had crossed paths with earlier that very day.

Was it possible to choose which past life we revisit in a regression session?

I recalled the lady conducting the previous regression session. Ironically, I was meeting her that same afternoon, which we had agreed to just a few days before after she unexpectedly extended her stay by another week. Turns out you can indeed choose which life to revisit, she told me, and with that my next regression session was booked in for later that week.

Meanwhile, I was also catching up with one of the other participants from the recent ceremony, wanting to learn more about her story and how the medicine path had found her. Unlike me, she was a seasoned professional when it came to working with the plant. Cacao was the medicine that had chosen her.

She told me about a ceremony in which the medicine itself told her not to come back until she embodied the lessons. That made me think:

What had the medicine given me, and did I listen?

It had freed me for sure, liberated me in many ways. But was I putting the chains that had fallen off me back on to myself? I could choose what I wanted to do now, and yet I felt like I was holding back somehow.

That thought lingering, I showered, got ready, and prepared food exactly the way I wanted it. I then went to a drumming festival, caught up with some friends, and didn't feel the need to fill in the gaps in conversation when two others joined us later that afternoon.

More importantly, I felt completely calm. No anxiety, no need to make conversation, but utterly content and comfortable in my own skin. It felt insanely satisfying not to 'have to' do anything. I could just be!

That's when I understood what the medicine had truly given me: the strength to not ignore the wisdom within. And also that, as much as she would give you her blessings, you still needed to put in the work yourself.

AT 6 a.m. sharp, due to the fact that we were on opposite sides of the world, I spoke to Ruby, the shaman/my next teacher I dreamed of after speaking to my parents following the ceremony. My friend told me not to have any expectations. Wise words, but difficult under these circumstances, when it felt like this conversation was a stepping stone into a completely different life.

I tried sitting in silence for a moment, listening to the wisdom of my body. There was a nervousness inside me, but in an excited kind of way. I felt joyous, my heart beating fast with possibility. Giddy, I switched on my laptop, ready to take that call.

We spoke for nearly an hour. She connected me to a local woman, and told me about her upcoming trip to sit with the Shipibo tribe two weeks from now.

In Peru.

My gut tightened as soon as she spoke those words and invited me to come along. I knew what I had to do.

The only problem? I had literally just returned to work after taking time off for Easter to spend time with my son, and work wasn't exactly flexible.

Peru.
A tribe.

The words kept echoing in my head.
Question after question followed quickly.

Could I do this with my son?

What she was suggesting was a nine-day dieta.

What would I tell work? And how about the riots in Peru? (The government had recently declared a state of emergency.)

It's worth mentioning that not once during this whole thought process did I stop to ask myself whether I was actually ready for the work she was proposing (something I highly recommend you do). The dieta was a nine-day process with the plant, and something that was usually only done by people who were a lot further down the track.

I took a deep breath and listened to my body. My heart was racing. It was a feeling difficult to describe—a deep yearning to go, and a knowledge that this would somehow help me find my new path.

I remembered how long I had waited for these doors to open, and now that they had, all I had to do was to say *Yes* and walk through.

Three hours later I had booked my tickets, filled out my travel authorisation, and made my down payment—knowing that if I didn't do it right away, I would talk myself out of it.

In less than a minute, I went from:

'*Fuck*! Am I actually *doing* this?'

To:

'OMG, I *am* really doing this!'

To:

'*FUCK*! I *AM* really doing this!'

I then spoke to my ex-husband, arranged childcare, and went from wanting to tell everybody to resolving to hold it close for the time being. I remembered the reading I had received in Bali years ago, before the doors to Peru closed for me for another six years, and how I asked for it again just a few days ago, promising that this time I would listen.

I debated what to say at work, when to tell my family, and also how much to share about it. The conversation at work seemed to be the biggest hurdle—until it wasn't. My whole being told me to just be honest: tell them that I had been given the opportunity of a lifetime, to sit with a native tribe in the Amazon. That I felt called to do it, and would regret it if I didn't. *Because I knew I would.*

With that, I submitted my holiday request. And then found my travel authorisation approval in my inbox seconds later.

The excitement didn't last very long—a few hours later, it was replaced with sheer terror. All of a sudden, I was petrified about the upcoming trip, and for good reason. After all, I am afraid of pretty much everything that resides in the Amazon. Thoughts of snakes, mosquitoes, and my general physical safety circled around my brain as I questioned my decision over and over again.

I tried to remind myself how guided this trip felt just a few hours earlier, and the unlikelihood of my teacher and I connecting under any other circumstances. It only helped so much.

But no matter the trepidation, given how close I was to my departure, I needed to get ready.

What does one wear in the Amazon?

Past-life regression session

I hardly slept the following night, plagued by visions of bugs, snakes, flies and mosquitoes. Tossing and turning, I tried to meditate in order to make sense of it all. Then, I remembered what my coach had said:

'It is an honour to be invited to Peru, and for those doors to open.'

I knew she was right, but that didn't make it any less scary.

With the upcoming trip and work, the past-life regression had completely slipped my mind until that very morning. What would it show me?

I had set the intention to go back to the shamanic life I was briefly shown during my integration session, and to remember my gifts from the past.

'The land remembers you,' the reader in Bali had told me back then.

But why? What for? And, maybe more importantly, did I still have it in me?

I should have asked all of these questions back then, but I didn't. Back then, I was a high-flyer in the corporate world, and shamanism and spirituality couldn't have been further from my very pragmatic, logical, 3D human experience.

In preparation for the regression session, I asked my spirit guides for support to help get me out of my head and see what I needed to see. Because as anxious as I was about what I was going to see, I had realised that what I was most afraid of was seeing nothing. Or, as the card I pulled that morning told me, dare to dream.

It was true—I was afraid to dream. Afraid of getting my hopes up and imagining the possibility, and afraid of the crash that followed if it wasn't the case.

'You're on the fast train now,' my coach had told me yesterday. A train going somewhere I didn't know, and one I didn't know how to stop.

Did I even want to stop it?

Part of me definitely didn't. My fear wanted to pull the brakes on fast. Ultimately, my curiosity won out.

Hoping that today would give me more answers, I jumped on the bus. That's when my nerves got the better of me. I felt like throwing up.

What if today showed my dreams were possible? My fantasy,
a reality?
 That everything I hoped for was true?

I hadn't allowed myself to go there before, instead look-ing at everything that could go wrong. But the sensation in my body today felt different. It was expecting, knowing—and equally afraid.

When I arrived, I spent a few minutes grounding myself outside, observing the fish in the pond until I became calm. Then, open to either possibility, accepting the duality of the situation, the light and the dark, I ascended the stairs to the allocated location.

The treatment room was light and beautiful, and had a very positive energy about it. After a quick intro from the past life regressionist about what to expect, I was guided into the hypnosis.

My role was simple: tell her everything I saw without judgement, as if it were in a movie. She would later make sense of it all. And so we began.

I saw myself walking through a golden gate, inside the room that
held the Akashic records. Multiple books were moving around
me, before a notepad landed in my arms. A feather came through
and I found myself writing something on a piece of paper.

'What are you writing about?' she asked me.

'Love,' I replied. (That could have referred to my first book, I later concluded, while hoping in that moment that that wasn't my only purpose.)

Next, I saw an eagle flying in the sky.

'What is below you?' she asked, but I couldn't tell.

'Try entering the eagle,' she suggested. I did. ('Not many people can do that,' she told me later.)

I saw valleys and trees and a whole landscape forming beneath me. A horse appeared in front of me. Wild, brown and with the cutest white little nose flash. It was running wild, happy and free.

A young Native American girl stepped forward, her hair plaited on either side.

'I am the chief's daughter,' I said to the instructor, seeing that vision very clearly.

'See if you can ride the horse,' she replied. I did.

No saddle, my hair flying wild in the wind, I started riding the horse. It felt so joyous!

'See if it can take you to the village,' she suggested. I could just make it out in the far distance.

That's when I realised I wasn't alone. Someone was riding beside me.

I recognised his energy before his face appeared. My heart strings pulled hard.

I would recognise this energy anywhere. It was the man I loved and had separated from just a few months ago.

I reached my hand out to him, and we held hands riding our horses.

He looked so happy and carefree—everything he was, apart from how I remembered him being lately.

I cried big tears at the vision, like I always did when he appeared in one of my visions. Like *he* always did, sooner or later.

The instructor gave me a moment to collect myself before I continued on to the next vision.

A memory of my son. He would have been less than two back then, riding his rocking horse across our living room. I recalled the moment, and saw myself excitedly cheering him on, teaching him how to ride it, not realising it was a distant memory of the past.

When he told me he loved me—in his own little language, before he could speak—I broke out in tears again.

He was my everything, then and now.

The memory vanished, and a teepee appeared, inviting me to enter.

A man was sitting in the middle of it, cross-legged like Buddha or a medicine man. He was holding a bead necklace in his hands, moving one bead after the other between his fingers.

(A vision that later connected me to Bhutan.)

I could hear the beat of a hand drum, and turned to see several people sitting on drums to the left of him, beating them loudly. My body started to move to the beat of the drum, and I saw myself throwing my hair back and forth carelessly. When the sound of the rattle joined in, a python appeared, and with it a wolf in the moonlight.

The wolf was one of my spirit guides, and has been ever since I was a little girl—my protector, showing me he was there to support me whenever it got hard.

The python slithered towards me slowly, circling around my legs until it was right in front of me. I wasn't afraid.

'Follow me,' it said. I followed the snake along the moonlit path.

'What else do you see?' the instructor asked.

'Water,' I replied, hesitantly.

'Go inside,' she said, telling me to wash everything off my body that was blocking me; anything that was holding me back.

I dunked underneath the water over and over again, faster and faster, until I finally slowed down.

'Take one final breath underneath the water before you resurface,' she told me. That was my rebirth, I later found out.

I came out of the water, dripping wet.

'How do you feel?' she asked, expecting me to feel strong and powerful.

'Wet and cold,' I answered, and then saw myself moving towards a fire.

Looking inside, I found myself burning inside it. Yet I didn't scream. Couldn't. Something told me that if I screamed, the fireball I had inside me would be released, and that couldn't happen.

'How do you feel?' she asked again. 'Angry?'

'Sad,' I replied, feeling tears running down my cheeks at the vision I had received.

The boy riding the horse with me had pushed me inside the fire.

I was betrayed. By someone I loved, and for something I strongly believed in.

She asked me to pause at this moment and go over to the young girl.

'Tell her everything you want to say,' she added, quietly.

I hugged the girl tightly. Told her that her life didn't go to waste. That I would finish whatever she started. Fulfil her purpose, and mine, whatever it looked like.

We then set her free. Together. After releasing everything that was in her throat, and mine.

A vision of my son's birth popped in. Then, too, I couldn't scream, and always said I wasn't a screamer.

As the instructor called me back from the meditation, the chief's daughter appeared in front of me one more time.

'Three, two, one…'

I heard the instructor count, as the chief's daughter integrated with my body.

'… and we're back.'

CHANGING BEHAVIOURS /
ADDRESSING NEEDS

WAS WAITING FOR my son to be dropped off at my place, after a week of silence from him. No text, no call, and only an odd-sounding conversation when I called.

This was unusual. We had always had a very strong relationship, and when he was with me, we pretty much talked all day. So before I continue, I really want to give him some credit—he is (by far!) the best thing that has happened to me and I do want to recognise how hard this situation would have developed for him in the meantime.

Something I learned to recognise only later. In that moment, I was just confused. I tried telling him in different ways that I'd love to hear from him more, that I missed him when he wasn't around, and that it made me sad when we didn't speak. But there was no progress, no change. It was as if I were talking to a brick wall.

Now what? The triggers in my body spoke very loudly in the meantime, as sadness, disappointment and hurt all hit me at once.

Not saying anything when he showed up wasn't an option. Having a go at him the second he walked through the door was not a great one either, and the silent treatment would be by far the worst.

How could I approach this the right way, respecting my boundaries as well as his? Standing in my authentic truth, while being compassionate with him?

After all, he was only twelve at the time—that tender age when parents are becoming uncool and friends more and more important, when the 'self' plays a much bigger role than anyone else, and when everything starts to change way too quickly. And also, deep down, I know that the silence doesn't mean he doesn't miss me, nor that he doesn't care—even if it's tempting to think otherwise.

So, how do I tell him where I'm coming from, so that he understands?

His dad tries telling me what I *shouldn't* do.

In the past, this would have triggered the crap out of me, and yet today I don't react.

I take my son out for a walk instead. At first, he is all grumpy about having to walk, since he's tired from a late night on the other side of the Bridge. But when I ask him to tell me about his week and listen intently, he tells me about it at great length.

I then asked him what happened when we spoke, and how he would have felt if he had tried to contact me to share something exciting, and I didn't respond. Especially if I sounded like I didn't even care.

He said he would probably be pretty upset by it. I agreed. I told him that I didn't want to be upset with him, and the options that went through my mind before he arrived.

He apologised. I thanked him for apologising, and then told him that I didn't share this with him to get an apology: I wanted to find a middle ground with him, one that worked for us both.

So, we brainstormed solutions together, negotiated how to make it work for both of us, and settled on speaking every two and a half days going forward. Now that was still not a lot, arguably, but it was two and a half days more than what we were doing right at that moment.

And with that, I later tuned off the lights and fell asleep, safe and sound.

Self-protection

Is the best self-protection being who you are, or hiding who you are?

A question I pulled out of a card deck that morning.

For many years, I believed it was hiding who I was. After all, it had kept me safe, and was by far the easier way to handle things—or so it felt.

What I didn't realise back then was that I was slowly losing myself along the way. Hiding wasn't self-protection, it was self-abandonment.

Knowing this now helped me realise that people won't always understand your path, or be by your side as you walk it. At times, that loss might feel unbearable. But the people who *will* stay in your life are the people who will show up for you, and the people you truly want in your life. Because they will love you *as you are*, for *who* you are, deep down inside.

It's funny how realisations work—this one came to me when I was at a crossroad with my bestie.

Old friendships, and new

That same evening, I caught up with a group of friends I made during the ceremony. I found myself surprised yet again by how quickly friendships could form when all parties were committed to doing the inner work.

Everybody's journey had unfolded differently. Some of us still had a lot of questions or resistance, while others felt inspired, and some of us could already feel the difference it had made in our lives—big time.

The night before, my journey had taken me to a drumming circle in Bondi, where I was asked to play with the other drummers as the sun came down. The only problem? I didn't know how to play!

My initial feeling when that vision first came through was disbelief. Why was I being shown that vision when I *knew* that I didn't know how to play the drum? Then my ego kicked in, not wanting me to be seen doing something I didn't know how to—especially not in front of a large crowd of people.

I meditated on my vision, and listened to a song that popped up on Spotify just as I was preparing for my meditation: 'You Guided Me', by Nessi Gomes.

As I was listening to the song, something fascinating happened: I saw myself playing the drum that afternoon—where I would be sitting and how, and how I would be playing the drum with my hands and fingers.

It was rolling in front of my eyes, like a movie on a giant screen. Nervously, I decided to trust that vision. I packed up the drum I had bought for my son a few years ago, and got ready to leave.

And then I did it. I marched over to the organiser the second we arrived, knowing my head would jump in if I didn't, and asked him if I could play with them that evening. I then found myself a seat in the corner of the drumming circle and started drumming just like I was shown in my vision: tentatively at first, and *very* conscious of the sounds it was releasing. I tried matching the rhythm of the others as much as possible, until I finally released control and went all in, pushing the vision to the back of my mind as much as possible.

I was no John Bonham that night, and it wasn't all perfect, but it also wasn't all bad. And, most importantly—it was actually a *lot* of fun!

Euphoric and proud (albeit with swollen fingers), I got home a few hours later, completely wiped.

The phone rang moments later, displaying my sister's number. I could feel a lump building in my throat instantly. Don't get me wrong, I *love* my sister (dearly!), and I want to have a good relationship with her—after all, we were best friends when I was back in Germany, until I messed things up when I moved to London.

But I wasn't ready to tell her about the journey yet, afraid of how she would respond and how this could impact the relationship we were still rebuilding. When I opened up to my ceremony friends about it, they helped me understand that I needed to slow down. Historically, I tended to over-share when I got excited, instead of allowing people to come on the journey with me gradually.

So, I picked up the phone, and shared just a little. To her credit, her reaction was as expected, but could have also been a *lot* worse!

Final blow

A few days later I heard the words no mother ever wants to hear—and it wasn't the dreaded 'I hate you' coming from a teenager.

Before I go into this chapter, I want to give my son some more credit. It's difficult navigating these changes at any point, let alone at his young age. The situation at home would have escalated without my knowing, and back then I was too naive to see what was coming my way—especially considering I played an instrumental role in accepting Nina's role with him in the first place, when they met. Now, back to the day...

My son and I were discussing his art project: a pillow he had designed at school. I was teasing him about when he was going to bring back '*my*' pillow, when the joke took a very unexpected turn. He told me the pillow was already at his dad's house, and that he had given it to Nina 'because she had taken him in and that was more important'.

'Than your mother?' I asked, surprised.

That came completely out of the blue. He nodded.

'She didn't have to do that,' he continued.

I agreed, but also pointed out it's not the same as raising him since he was little.

'*Especially* since I'm not *her blood*!' he declared.

I was gobsmacked. 'Is that truly how you feel?' I asked, taken aback by his conviction.

Seeing my reaction, he asked why I was making such a big deal about a pillow.

I told him I couldn't care less about the pillow. *Not my proudest moment.*

The following morning was really emotional, as I tried balancing being an adult and being deeply hurt. Tears kept coming to the forefront, and I didn't want to ignore them. 'How can I be compassionate with him *and* with myself?' I asked myself over and over.

Guide me in this conversation, I begged, yet got nothing in return.

I started preparing my son's breakfast, and then went on to make his lunch.

'Can I have a hug?' he asked as he entered the kitchen area.

'Of course,' I said, clearing the dishes from the sink.

I knew it was what he needed for his nervous system, even though it wasn't what I needed for mine. Physical touch is my love language, and after the conversation we had had the night before, a hug was the last thing on my mind.

That hug cracked me open even more.

I made tea and went on to do the dishes. *How should I handle this?* I asked myself, scrubbing the plates in the sink. Every option I could think of didn't feel right.

Should I show him how much what he said had upset me? Or would I be downloading my nervous system onto his?

He came into the kitchen once more as I was throwing out the flowers, trying to keep myself busy with anything I could.

'Do you want a hug?' he asked this time.

'Sure,' I replied, even though I was far from sure. But still, I knew that a child shouldn't have love taken away from them as a punishment.

'I'm sorry,' he told me inside the embrace.

'For what?' I asked.

'For saying two years are more important than twelve,' he replied.

'That's your reality,' I replied. 'I'll just need some time to accept that.'

I started to cry. 'I understand it's not easy for you, balancing two homes,' I continued, 'and you are in a very fortunate position where we both love you *so* much; that Dad found someone who cares for you so deeply. But for someone who loved you *all* your life, that's a very hard pill to swallow.'

He nodded, and left the kitchen cheerfully. For him, this conversation was over.

But for me, this was anything but done. I had stopped myself. I had done what I always did, *the right thing*, but it didn't feel right, and that was not okay. At the risk of my inner child coming out screaming loudly, I followed him into the living room.

'I don't know who taught you that,' I started slowly, 'but no one is more important than Mum. And Dad,' I added. 'There will be times when you will be closer to Nina, times when you will feel I don't understand you. But there is only one mother.'

I paused. 'That doesn't take away anything that Nina does for you. She does a great job helping Dad raise you. Raising you.' I paused again.

'Like there is no one who will ever replace my mother,' I added, and told him about the time I was asked to call my mother-in-law 'Mother' due to local traditions. Back then, I had really struggled with that concept. I told him about the moments I really didn't get on with *my* mother, and the times we completely disagreed—but also that she was still my mother, regardless.

I realised this wasn't about me and Nina any longer. I wasn't competing with her or comparing us in any way. This was me believing in myself and standing up for the mother within me. Believing in *her* power and strength.

'This is something for me to think about while I'm in Peru,' I concluded, 'and maybe something for you to think about while I'm gone.'

He nodded, brushed his teeth, put on his shoes, and went out the door.

I could see there was a lesson in this for me, somewhere— saw the power of standing up for what I believed in and of standing in my authenticity as I just did. It felt good. *Right.* Like I finally had done *the right thing*, for me. And that feeling was unbelievable.

May—preparing for travel

I was dreaming of the jungle pretty much every night now, likely because my trip was merely five days away.

One night, I saw myself running through the jungle searching for a white drum; the next, a leopard was guiding me towards it. The past few nights were about being unable to establish a connection while I was there, the land not remembering me and the medicine not working, full stop.

I dreamed of the shaman doing an initiation, and of the one I sat with during the last ceremony. Finally, I dreamed of my family sitting around the kitchen table, discussing something I was unable to hear.

I woke up and took pen to paper. It was time to set my intentions for the 'retreat'.

Road to recovery

I was on my third intention letter. The more I wrote, the more real it got, and yet the more questions it raised.

My second attempt had been mostly questions:

Why did the chief's daughter integrate with me, and how can I unlock her?

Why was I told to go to Peru, and why does the land remember me?

How do I step into my purpose, and what do I need to learn?

What is my power and what don't I see?

The third attempt felt more like praying:

Release me from my suffering,

Show me what caused it, and help me move past it. Open my eyes and ears.

Help me see what's missing and hear what I don't.

Quite timely to all of this, I was invited to a sunrise cacao ceremony by the medicine woman I had met a few weeks ago. My friend and I joined her at the beach, just as the sun came out.

The spot she had chosen was decorated with candles, flowers and leaves. As she poured us the cacao, she told us the history of the changing moon. We set our intentions, and she handed us an oracle card each, to guide us through our journey clockwise, north to north. Each direction would represent a season, showing us the journey that lay upon us along the way.

I had never done anything like that before, and was surprised by how many insights I received. But first, my oracle took me back to the very beginning. As I laid my card down facing north, it showed me my childhood in Germany, and the obstacles I overcame. My time in the UK came up next, where—following these lessons from home—my willpower emerged.

From there, the medicine woman guided me onto my journey ahead, showing me that it was that same willpower I would be required to have once more, and very soon. I was told to expect the first part to be wobbly, and that I would be unclear about what it all meant, but that soon I would be braver, understand the path better, and dive deeper into the learnings of the plant.

At that point, Lauren, the lady with the parking ticket, would become more present in my life again, teaching me what I needed to learn, before my neighbour would step forward, connecting the community.

I would then come full circle again and back to my being, connecting to spirit more deeply, before giving birth to another child.

The night before take-off

I had the weirdest dream that night. This time I wasn't in the jungle, and yet it felt way too close to home. Everything I wanted to eat was too expensive, and the house I owned was no longer there. My son and I broke into a house, before I woke up confused and rattled.

Was my career change playing more on my mind than I thought?
Was it a blind spot I was trying to ignore?

Real life, on the other hand, wasn't much better. It would be Mother's Day during my stay in Peru, and I was gutted to be missing it. My son looked at it rather positively: he'd spend the day with Nina, he told me, and 'it would be the same.'

It broke my heart hearing those words come out of his mouth. I tried explaining the difference to him once more later that night, and again in the morning, failing miserably both times—or so it felt.

We said goodbye on very shaky grounds, and yet soon after he left for school that day, I knew that this was exactly the way it was meant to happen. Truth was the theme for my journey—now, and then.

WITH THAT in mind, I packed the final items for my flight.

THE JOURNEY BEGINS

I WAS AT THE airport, waiting for my flight to board in the next hour, surprised by how calm I was. Or maybe I was just too tired, as I had barely had three hours of sleep.

Luckily, the days in the lead-up to this were full of self-care. I had washed all of my clothes, bedding and towels, cleaned everything I wanted to take with me, and left the house as spotless as I could. Knowing I would return a different person, I wanted to make it my personal 'welcome home' to the version to come.

Thirty-two hours later, we were ready to descend into Lima. This was it—the official first step of the journey, and where I would meet at least two of the other participants. It was getting *real*.

Up until that moment, I had been waiting for something to go wrong: for my PCR results to be delayed, for any missing documents to pop up, my luggage to disappear, or for someone to stop me somewhere along the way. But, apart from a minor delay out of Sydney, it had all gone very smoothly. *Too* smoothly for my liking—especially when even the customs agent in L.A. took out his phone and showed me pictures from *his* recent trip to Peru after learning where I was headed. *It was unreal*!

Unlike now, when everything was becoming *very* real all of a sudden. I was a combination of excitement and nervousness, filled with anticipation and a thousand questions.

Had I done enough?
Focused on the right things?

I finally started thinking about the actual journey, as well. So far I had only considered the experience in the jungle, but now the bit of knowledge I had of what was to come suddenly pushed to the front of my thoughts.

I had never done a dieta before, and if one experience was able to bring up so much, what would four ceremonies with the master plant and three with an assigned plant bring?

I had accepted that mosquitoes and devil-fly bites were part of the experience, and prepared for non-stop itching. I was ready for the 'stuff' that would come through the mosquito net, and the noises of the jungle at night; become mentally ready to live with an Indigenous tribe without speaking their language; and was ready to trust someone I had never met before. Yet the drum kept playing on my mind.

Where would I find it? In Lima? Pucallpa? L.A.?

'The universe will provide', I was told in the last reading. But if this was going to be my healing tool, I really didn't want to miss it.

That, and my shamanic tattoo would make the trip worthwhile, I decided. Shallow, I know, considering the wisdom I had before me, but the heart wants what it wants, and somehow, having something physical and visible would somehow make the experience more real and believable for me.

'There's no place for logic' was echoing through my ears as I walked towards the gate to meet the others—another thing I had been told in my energy healing session just before I left. Easier said than done, though, when you've lived in your head for so many years. But I was willing to try.

THE LAST plane to Pucallpa was delayed, stretching the forty-one-hour journey to forty-three. By then, I was dying for a hot shower and a bed—not necessarily in that order.

My heart was racing when we flew over the valley. 'The land remembers you' kept echoing in my ears. *Would it*?

I had met some of the participants at the airport before we boarded the plane, so this would officially be the last leg of solitude before the journey began—and it was very much appreciated, as jet lag was starting to hit me hard.

My mind, on the other hand, was occupied by the message I had found on my phone just before take-off, which had caused a whirlwind of emotions almost instantly.

I hadn't heard from Jimmy—the man I was in love with—in nearly six months, and now, as it turned out, he too was planning a trip to the Amazon. *For the same reason*?

In his message, he said he had thought about my family these past few months, and of my son in his first year of high school. That he hopes I'd been very well too.

In hindsight, it was probably a very nice message. But at the time, I had to put it away. Not because I didn't care—on the contrary, I sometimes thought I cared too much—but because this trip wasn't about him. *Unlike the past two years.*

I didn't want to give the message more credit than necessary, even though I *had* to open it as soon as I saw its notification and *needed* to know what he said before I boarded that plane.

He sounded happy about my trip, but didn't ask any questions. Didn't tell me that he missed *me*, too. Maybe this was meant to be implied—I was never good at reading between the lines when it came to romance.

Instead, I stuffed my phone back in my bag.

This would have to wait.

Jungle here we come!

In three hours, we would be on the boat that would take us five hours down the Ucayali River, deep into the rainforest. I had been up for hours.

After I showered, moisturised and played music, Jimmy's message came back to my mind. I didn't want to leave him hanging for eleven days, knowing that I wouldn't have electricity or Wi-Fi until I got back, but I also didn't want to spend the next eleven days thinking about it either.

First, I told him where I was going and why, and that if he felt the same calling, he should go. Soon.

Good! That felt strong. Showing him this trip wasn't about him (just because of his text), but about me and my future.

Next, I sent a message to my sister, apologising for not being there for her seventeen years ago, and then I told my friends how much I loved them—everyone who was playing a big role in my life at that time.

Then I came full circle, realising I had just told everyone how much I cared about them, with the exception of the person who meant the most to me, apart from my son.

It was a funny feeling not knowing what to expect or what was about to come. Not knowing *how* I would come back, or *if*—as I wasn't completely oblivious to the dangers I was exposing myself to in staying with an Indigenous tribe.

So, I told Jimmy that he was my emergency contact. Showing him that even after all this time, my love for him hadn't changed. And that, when it came down to it, he still was the person I wanted to know first. *Because he was.*

I then re-packed my bags, zipped them up tightly, and headed out for the adventure of my life. Knowing that, for the next eleven days, I wouldn't get a reply and that this was where I had to leave it all behind.

Mother's Day

We went to the docks and patiently waited for our boat to arrive, tickets in hand. A local man sang passionately into his karaoke machine, surrounded by a milling crowd of people carrying bags, boarding their vessels, selling goods or buying tickets. It felt strange being in civilisation for the last time and not being able to communicate; it made the experience ahead feel all the more daunting.

Moments later, our bags were placed on top of our boat, and we were on our way.

The boat stopped every hour or so to let people on and off, giving the residents an opportunity to sell their food and drinks. Houses and other signs of civilisation started disappearing the further we coasted down the river. I was sitting next to Ruby, the woman responsible for my trip to Peru, while the other participants spread across the boat.

As we moved further along, there was a noticeable shift in all of us. Everyone suddenly became very quiet and thoughtful, our respective internal dialogues running through our minds as we looked at the outskirts of the jungle from our little window.

What will this journey bring?

The thought of this being my home for the next eleven days was overwhelming.

Why did it take me here?
And what would it show me?

I was a mix of anticipation and anxiety.

A few hours into the journey, Ruby started telling me about her last trip to the jungle, and how everything changed for her as a result. How *she* had changed first, and then turned everything around thereafter—her business, and her relationships. To her, this trip felt like coming home. To me, it was a gateway to the unknown.

I sat outside on the front deck for a while, watching the river merge with the horizon. It was mind-blowing to see the sheer size of it. Two thousand and seven hundred kilometres long—it was larger than anything I had ever seen before, stretching far and wide in every direction. And yet it felt really peaceful somehow—that is, if one could ignore the sounds of the horror movie that was playing on the TV inside the cabin, which had replaced the pop music channel and its half-naked artists. The contrast was surreal, but somehow all part of the experience, highlighting the distance between our current world, and where we were headed.

Ali, another member of our group, sat down next to me for a while and we basked in the sunshine, before the driver called us back inside and told us to get ready, as we would be getting off at the next station. Suddenly, the journey became very tangible for all of us.

It was hot when we arrived. Our bags were carried off the boat and dropped onto the muddy ground next to a tuktuk, which would later take us inside the little village. The village children were watching us curiously, from a safe distance.

I wondered how many people like us came here each year, and what the children would make of us.

What did it teach them?
What were they told?

Inside the village, which would become my home for the next eleven days, we were assigned our tambo, a small single-room dwelling on stilts, and had a lunch consisting of rice, peas and fish. Fish, we learned, was a delicacy to celebrate our arrival; the following days would be mostly vegetarian.

We also learned this would be our first and only meal for the day, since we would be having our first ceremony that same night. That wasn't the original plan, but since it was Mother's Day here the following day, the locals were preparing for a big celebration.

Unclear of my intentions for the day and what to prioritise, the list I created before I left was making hula hoops inside my mind.

Anxiously, I settled inside my tambo and lit a candle. I then journaled frantically, as if my life depended on it. Ready or not, it was time to face the maloca.

Let the games begin!

It was a big ceremony for me that night—bigger than I could have ever anticipated, or dared to imagine. When I entered the maloca around 8 p.m., still unsure of the energies of our group, I was confronted with the energy of seven others. Turns out we weren't the only people in the village at that time.

The mat I had originally chosen turned out to be occupied by someone else. I found my items spread across another mattress by the door—the one place I *didn't* want to sit, after my previous experience in a similar position.

The shaman came inside about thirty minutes later. By then I had accepted the situation with my mat, and understood it was teaching me to let go of control.

Unlike in my last ceremony, the shaman didn't see us one-on-one before we started, and there was no cleanse or preparation: just silence and darkness, as he lay down in the middle of the room and started puffing his tobacco in every direction.

He was facing away from me, making it even harder to read what was happening in the room, while a supporter of his went around placing the medicine inside our cups.

The liquid was thick and gooey, and extremely hard to swallow. I tried my hardest to keep it down as long as possible, while waiting in silence and anticipation for what was about to come. When the journey began, supported by music from the villagers, the shaman began to sing his Icaros and chants.

A big portion of my night was about my son—showing me my place in his life and why he chose me as his mother. The words:

'I AM HIS <u>ONLY</u> MOTHER'

rang loudly in my ears.

So loud I wasn't sure if it was for me or him at first. But the message came through so strong and powerful that it sank deep inside my core. I've never questioned it since.

Then, the plant reminded me once more of his earthly connection, and told me to connect him to my deep knowledge of the plants.

My sister came through next, showing me that expectations needed to go both ways. That message sank in deeply too.

I then got to heal my anger and hold myself for times I needed to be loved, shown to allow men to look after me again, and that this was something they liked doing, so not to push them away when they did.

The biggest portion was about Jimmy, where, at the end of the night, I was asked to commit to him as my husband. Now this was a big one for me, since I didn't plan on ever getting married again, at the time.

I want to pre-empt here that what was shown to me with Jimmy was an illusion of mine, I later got to uncover—the hard way. As you will see throughout the next pages, it ended up being a very painful lesson to learn—differentiating 'want' from reality.

So again, for anybody embarking on this journey, please practise discernment—especially (but not exclusively) when it comes to the topic of love. What happens when you don't will be illustrated throughout the next chapters.

In the second part of my journey, I got to release all negativity against Nina. The medicine called for me to sit with 'That sucks', instead of pretending everything was okay, like I usually did. To truly acknowledge it and let it go. (That part, comparatively, was very healing, then and now.)

The honesty in that was *unreal*, and more liberating than I could have imagined.

Lastly, I got to let go of judgements. I surprised myself by how much I had stored up, and opened my heart to more compassion. I was told to trust in myself and in my guidance, and that in moments of darkness, there would always be support. (Almost like for Harry Potter.)

My body emptied itself in every direction that night, as I released all negativity. It was all part of the package I had signed up for, I guess.

When I left the maloca at five in the morning, I was astounded by how much had happened in one night alone. This would give me a month's worth of stuff to think about, if I wanted to implement it all (the most important part of working with the medicine). And yet this was only day one of the experience...

What had I just signed up for?

The following day was the official start of our dieta, meaning that the shaman would allocate our assigned master plant to us, and open the dieta through chants later that night. I woke up with the rising sun and went for a walk.

It was quiet as I walked alongside the river, with only a few birds circling above. Passing an area of tall grass, I was startled by a rustling noise. In the past, I would have judged the hell out of myself for being such a scaredy cat, and told myself to get a grip. *Not today.* Today, I held myself with love and compassion until I calmed myself.

Once I settled down, I thought about my situation with Nina. I was happy to take responsibility for not setting boundaries earlier, but not for what she had done—even though I could better understand now *why* she'd done it, which was a big moment for me.

So I was reading *The Road Less Travelled* by M. Scott Peck, which had helped me finally understand why I was the way I was. While influenced by others, that too now was my problem to solve—the book had only shown me its origin. And I also learned that expecting the other party to heal your wound on your behalf means giving away your power once more. Instead, it was time I healed myself. This likely ended up being the most profound part of my healing journey, and something I lean on very heavily up until today.

Speaking to one of the other participants on my way back to my tambo, I found out about the local healer of the village—who was able to check your organs' health and energetic field through touch—as well as a herbalist prescribing cleansing nuts, which were called vomitido and cleansed you from parasites and more.

I wasn't exactly excited by the prospect of emptying myself for several hours, but the moment I was told about them, I knew I had to consult both the healer and the herbalist. After all, healing was what I'd come here for, and the effects of the vine only increased the cleaner the body was—or so I'd been told.

During breakfast, I connected with another participant and told him about a book I had written just before I got here. Then, he told me that he was a film director from the States. *What were the odds?*

Journaling on this later, I got a sense that he might be directing a film of my book later down the track, so I went over to his tambo and asked if he was open to reading it. He told me he had been just about to ask me if he could. My heart started racing super-fast.

Was this what had brought me here?

A few hours later we were sitting opposite Papa Guilberto, the last-known shaman of his lineage, waiting for him to allocate our plant.

I was given Noya Rao, the tree of light and the plant I initially felt very drawn to—up until I dreamed that Bobinsana should be my first plant, and Noya Rao my second. My first reaction was disappointment: all that day I had a feeling this would be my allocated plant, and that I would have to fight for them to come in the right order. I didn't.

When the shaman allocated my plant, I spoke up, but did not fight for it: it just felt incredibly wrong to disrespect the maestro. And yet, as soon as we left the circle, I regretted my decision.

I found the organiser and asked him for guidance. He recommended sitting by the Bobinsana tree with an offering, asking for guidance as I did.

And so I did, with no result. Turns out there is a right (and wrong) way to give an offering, and I clearly didn't get it right. I got nothing. Not even when I asked the chief's daughter for support.

I felt torn.

Had I just made a mistake?

A fellow participant suggested that I 'just listen to my guidance', but which one? The one I trusted the longest, or the man who did this for a living?

I knew this couldn't be solved with logic, so I went to the local healer instead. This would be the last chance I would have to see him, since once our dieta opened, all forms of physical touch were strictly forbidden. No touching, no hugging, and as little eye contact as possible.

I stepped inside the healer's home/workplace, where little children and chickens circled around us curiously. Pulling out a rug thinner than a yoga mat, he asked me to undress.

He had inherited the power of Noya Rao from his father when he passed, I learned from one of the other participants who I had asked to join me for translation purposes—it was apparently the only way this knowledge could be achieved.

As I lay on the floor, he got to work. His touch was experienced, his hands moving up and down my body with confidence. I had bad energy in my back, I was told, and that Papa would take care of it during ceremony, before a dislocated rib was pushed back inside my rib cage. To say that this was unexpected would be an understatement; I would also be lying if I said it didn't hurt.

He continued working on my body, my eyes, my neck, and my lower back. The eyes were excruciatingly painful. I asked Ali to translate why they felt this way.

'Too many hours in front of the computer,' was the reply. How he knew that was beyond me, since I hadn't shared with the group what I did for work. Guess I wasn't the only one who came here with that problem.

The pressure was pushing down from my forehead onto my eyes, neck and lower back, he continued. I hadn't told him about my neck pain either.

Literally crawling out of the healer's dwelling after he had finished, I felt both relieved and thoughtful. I was ready for whatever the dieta had in store for me that night.

Or so I thought.

MOMENTS AFTER I had my second cup, Papa Guilberto opened the space by singing chants to our individual plants in the middle of the ceremony.

I wish I had known about this beforehand. Halfway through his chants, I started to feel *really* nauseated. We were sitting in a small circle, and as much as I tried to hold it in and not purge in front of all the other participants, I just couldn't. Luckily, I wasn't the only one—although I guess that's a matter of perspective.

Once he finished the group chants, Papa then sang to us individually, and sealed each of us with Mapacho protection.

The medicine felt different from the one I had experienced the night before, and didn't have half of the same effect for me, which made my journey pretty eventless—if not a little dull, to some degree.

For a while I saw dark energies circling around me, trying to enter my body, but then everything just disappeared, and I was left in nothingness. No messages, no insights—simply a night spent in the maloca observing everyone else's journeys.

I took the second cup, but apart from making me purge, it had little effect. So, I put the night down as a cleanse rather than a journey, and accepted it for what it was. One of the other participants, however, was having a *really* hard time, and watching her without being able to comfort her was a lot harder than I expected.

Becoming radically honest

The next morning, we were told to start observing our feelings as if they were a separate entity. I had my first opportunity to do so when a new girl arrived later that day.

I found her behaviour incredibly triggering at first, which fasting for half of the day only amplified. The way she spoke and acted felt incredibly insincere—a trait I had observed in others before. I thought of its origins, and a friend of mine popped to mind.

Was that what had caused the recent disconnect between us?

The second moment came when I offered to bring my essential oils to the group, as an additional ingredient for the perfume we were making. Walking over to the others, I found myself judging them hard, imagining one of the participants in particular disapproving of my oils quite strongly. It came out of nowhere, and triggered me just thinking about it. I had been judging my oils, like I was judging everything about myself—thinking that they weren't good enough, fearing the disapproval of the others.

In the end everyone loved them, her included, and highlighted once more just how much I still needed to prove myself to others, and what I was here to let go of.

Bottoms up!

I felt very calm and floaty, yet also very clear somehow—at least up until that horse bug bit me, snapping me back to reality again quickly. Itching, I made my way over to the shaman for my first cup of Noya Rao. *Enlightenment, here I come!*

They say the plant first communicates with you through dreams, and that everyone's experience can be very different. My first dreams on Noya Rao were utterly confusing, ranging anywhere from family relations, to food, to futuristic machinery. The underlying theme of Germany was at its centre.

I got really cold at one stage, tossing and turning in bed, and got up to put another throw on. The sleep was gone. Heavy-headed and confused, I got up a little later, trying to understand what it all meant.

I WAS guided to pull a card from the soul seeker deck later that morning, asking me what I would do if I could choose *anything* in the world.

I had read this card once before and recalled not being able to answer it. This time, my answer was easy:

I want to be the healer I was shown I could be in the first ceremony.

(A very common vision, by the way.)

What I didn't recall was that the card had two more questions on it: *Why* I wanted it, and *to what extent.*

'Why' was easy: because it felt good! More than good—right! Like life finally made sense. As if I had found something that I *wanted* to do—and, even more, who I wanted to *be.* I remembered my promise to the chief's daughter and corrected myself: what *we* wanted to do.

'To what extent?' She burned for it. Not that I wanted to go to that length necessarily, but I had come all the way to the Peruvian jungle to find my answer.

I realised there and then that I would go much further than that to live out our truth.

From pink dolphins to anacondas, devil flies and skulls on rivers ...
the Amazon reflects both life and death;

It cures you through its healing wonders, and also brings you to your knees.

It humbles, nurtures and surrounds you, and shows you where before went wrong.

Then mends you, grounds you and embraces you ... so you can come back to the world all strong.

Yet that next pass is new beginning, a chance to live a life that's pure.

It's not a pass to do more evil, as it will catch up with you at last ...

Take with you all you gained in knowledge—and share it, don't be shy to do.

Let then it stretch beyond its powers, and heal not you, but the whole world.

CHAPTER 4

BACK AT HOME

SPOKE TO MY boss last night and told her I was leaving my job. It was a message I had received loud and clear during my last couple of days in the jungle.

It was a scary step to take, leaving a senior director role behind to march into the unknown. I want to emphasise here that this was not the result of one ceremony, but something I had known and seen coming for a number of years (seven, give or take). Knowing it was time was the missing link before. But as I was asked during my travels, I was going to replace *knowing* with *faith*.

The conversation went as well as it could have done. She wasn't pleased, of course, given it was my first day back at the office. She even offered me a part-time solution, but I declined.

I always knew I wanted to do something meaningful in my life, and being in Peru made it really hit home. Seeing how people were healed physically, mentally and emotionally, and being part of their journeys, made all I was doing seem of little worth in comparison. I prided myself on a fancy title and region, and the healthy salary that came with it, but in the grand scheme of things, *what was I truly doing*?

What impact was I having? When I looked back at my life twenty or thirty years from now, would I feel proud of what I had achieved? Or would I look back knowing I dared to dream of something so much bigger, of leaving a very tangible impact on someone's life?

Whatever is to come, it feels right to be doing it. So, here's to daring bravely, and the next mountain to climb!

Two days later

I dreamed of snakes again that night. Lots of them. I knew they were surrounding me and knew exactly where they were, even though I couldn't see them.

I was at the estate I was booked to go to in September. The dream focused on the future, showing me how everything I had done up until now was about the past, and that the next chapter would be about what was to come. *Naturally.* Is it even possible to look ahead without looking back?

Meanwhile, I was preparing to hand in my written notice at work, and while yesterday it had felt so right to have taken this step, today the reality of it started to really sink in. It was different from doubt, because I still didn't question that it was the right decision, and yet the unknown was really hitting home.

Everything else in my life seemed to have changed since I returned as well. My relationship with my son was visibly different from what it had been. It was as if I was able to see him for who he truly was for the first time, and accept him as my equal as a result. As noted before, we are all mirrors...

The difference in myself was also quite telling. No longer was I questioning my role in his life—instead, I stepped into the mother role more than ever before. As strange as it sounds, I even started enjoying the small tasks more than ever. Cooking for him, looking after him—things that had previously felt like chores now felt like a privilege.

I thought about it as I was preparing breakfast that morning. In the past I would have opted for quick and easy choices, for both of us. Now, I was getting up extra-early to cook him something nice and put extra effort into his lunch box. Even more than I did before, I would try to think of all the other things I could add to ensure he had the best possible day.

I then thought about how much more of this I *could* do, once I was no longer in my role. Working late nights and being up with him early hadn't been the best recipe for success. Sure, there would be stressful times again in the future—I had no illusions about that—but if I continued the path of inner work, I would be able to shift with the changing times much faster going forward, especially now that my son was becoming a teenager.

That brought me to my next point: I needed to figure out what I was going to do in the future.

Contemplating my options, I thought of friends who had become self-employed. They all had one thing in common: each of them had a modality. *What was mine?*

Writing popped back into my mind. I enjoyed writing immensely, and yet struggled to identify with it fully. After I had told the film director about my day job during the dieta, he asked if he could think of me as a writer. I agreed, and yet didn't fully step into that role until many years down the line. Maybe it was because it didn't feel like it would be the *only* thing I would be doing; or because I also wanted to be the healer I was shown I could be while I was in Peru.

I thought back to the medicine woman I met in the jungle, who within days of our stay cured the leg of a limping participant. What did I have to show in comparison? I shouldn't compare, of course, but this wasn't a 'I want to have what you have' type of comparison, but rather a 'we have the same hours in the day' comparison. How was I spending mine, when this was what the world truly needed?

I thought back to how many people get to experience Papa Guilberto's magic: three hundred and fifty lucky souls in a year, to be precise. I knew because I had asked that question after having had the privilege of being one of them.

It was amazing what he did, especially considering how many years he'd already spent doing it. Yet it was a drop in the ocean compared to how many people need his help in this life. *Our* help, I should clarify, considering how quickly the suicide rates are climbing, and how much younger victims have started to become.

That spurred me to want to do more, *be* more—to give back in all the ways I have received. Not just in Peru, but my whole life. To use the riches I have known in order to enable others.

The book *The Life You Can Save* popped into my mind, in which the author, Peter Singer, asks you to calculate how much you truly need, suggesting all else should be donated to someone who needs it more. It reminded me of how good it had felt to have been able to help a friend out financially after I returned, as well as saying 'Yes' to supporting the family of a little girl in Peru by paying for her hospital visit.

So, yes, I might not have a job two months from now, but I *do* have my health, a robust support network, a roof over my head, and a hot meal and shower every single day. And with that, it suddenly became easy handing in my notice that week.

It was time for me to step into the light.

Unfinished business

My neighbour's girlfriend created a WhatsApp group called 'Coogee friends' for the three of us, in which she asked about my trip to Peru.

My body responded instantly. They say the body knows first, and mine gave me a definite 'don't go there'. We were anything *but* friends, and the way we had left things before my travels was anything but friendly. (I had met with her and her father, following her request, with little result.)

That remembrance was followed by a clear message to stay true to myself. I didn't reply.

As expected, I found an array of messages from her on my phone twelve hours later, in which she told me she was going away for three weeks and didn't want to see me anywhere near her boyfriend. She told me to call a handyman if my window broke; go someplace else if I needed a massage; stay away from her partner; and that she didn't want to hear that I had had a glass of wine alone with him on a Friday or Saturday night, because she didn't feel comfortable with me. 'Sorry' (quote), but she just didn't.

Lastly, she mentioned that he had told her I was flirting with him when they were on the rocks—which wasn't nice coming from another woman.

I sat with that for quite a few moments. Firstly, I wouldn't dream of getting a massage from my neighbour—that would be beyond awkward. Secondly, I hadn't had alcohol in over seven weeks, and I wasn't planning to anytime soon, with or without him. Lastly, what she accused me of was simply untrue.

It took me a moment to formulate my response:

> *'Emily, you have got to stop—enough with the accusations and those messages. It is completely uncalled for. If you don't trust me, you should at least trust your boyfriend. As I told you before, I am not interested in him that way. Now please leave me be and enjoy your holiday.'*

It took her a few days to respond, during which a number of things happened simultaneously. There was a long exchange with my sister, who struggled to understand my decision to leave the corporate world. There were more dreams about my drum, as well as an exchange with Jimmy—the man I was still in love with. I could understand where my sister was coming from, especially in hindsight, but I also couldn't keep justifying my decision. At that time, my family`s attempts to protect me translated to angst and paranoia on my end, making me question my decision to share it with them prematurely.

I contemplated staying away for a little bit to let the dust settle, but if I'd learned anything from the past, it was that distance rarely made things better—or did it? I didn't want to run away from what was ahead of me, and neither did I want to ignore what needed to be said. Instead, I wanted to stay true to myself and my beliefs, something I didn't do enough growing up. This time, I wanted to address it head on.

Meanwhile, the dreams about my drum continued, after I set an intention for it the previous evening. The drum looked different in my dream compared with the one I saw at a festival that same afternoon, and yet when I started playing it, joy filled my entire body. I saw myself touching it with the curiosity of a little kid—yearning to play it, humming a little song as I walked. It gave me hope it was still out there, waiting for me. It was there, somewhere, with my name written all over it.

Then, I received a message from Jimmy. My heart jumped a beat when I saw it. We had been texting on and off since I arrived back from Peru. He told me how brave my step was, and asked me how I felt. Surprisingly, he and the film director I met in Peru were the only two people who had actually asked me that question.

I told him it felt right in every part of my body, and yet I spent all my time justifying my decision. That I was afraid—of the consequences this would have on my son, my situation with Nina, and of jumping into the unknown. Plus, there was guilt towards my team and company, leaving them as I did. But there still wasn't a question in my mind that I *had* to do this—the same way my body knew 'not to go there' with the WhatsApp message just a day before.

With that, I exited the group that Emily had created. I couldn't keep living in fear.

I WENT for a run the following morning; twenty-five minutes along the beach. My body felt weak, my mind overloaded. Snippets of conversations entered my mind, followed quickly by moments of determination.

I thought about where I was with my family in relation to my work, how life was shaping up overall, and reconfirmed the promise I gave in Peru. I was running fast at that point, my footsteps echoing loudly as they pounded the pavement.

As I was coming to the end of the run, I received a visual of myself swimming in the sea. It was not something I had planned or prepared for. I looked around. Feeling the icy water touching my feet, I spotted some people here and there, but fewer towards the end of the beach. A blessing, considering I didn't have a swimsuit.

I walked to the far end, took off my pants, and considered my underwear. Yep, just as I thought—anything but beach-appropriate. Then, I dove in. The water was cold and refreshing, sucking me in as if I was its own. It was *exhilarating*! It made me appreciate the guidance I had received, and the goodness that came with it when I followed it.

That's when I allowed myself to completely indulge in it. I dived under a wave, took my body in and out of the water and fully embraced it.

When I got out, I dried myself with my T-shirt and put on my pants and jumper. My underwear in hand, I marched towards the exit. I felt *amazing*!

Until I glanced at my phone and found another message from Emily. This one wasn't pleasant—not that the other ones particularly were, either.

'Perfect. And don't use excuses like your window or other minimal things to get close to him. I know what you are doing. Things were complicated with me and him and I think you were trying things to get closer to him (he thinks this as well).

So please stay far. I don't like you around him and I don't feel comfortable, he knows already.

I will have an amazing trip but always keeping an eye'

First of all, her grammar was atrocious—it took every ounce of my willpower to not correct her. I know, probably not what I should have been focusing on right then, but it really bugged me. I took a deep breath, trying to find the right words to say. A balance between speaking my mind, and not being horrible. That was the promise I gave returning from the Amazon. So, I wrote the following:

'Emily, do you hear yourself? I don't know where these insecurities are coming from, but you need to look within. I know it's easier to outsource your problems onto someone else, but the problems in your relationship are not my doing. I am not the cause and will not take this on. Neither will I let you tell me what I can and can't do, who I can and can't call and who I get to be friends with. That's my decision. And your boyfriend's, if he so chooses. So, for everyone's sake, find peace within yourself on that trip and point your eyes inwards. You will be surprised by what you find.

I then sent a message to my neighbour, telling him about the messages I was receiving and asking him to leave me out of their relationship. Next, I sent a message to Jimmy.

Later that afternoon, I went to support my coach at the MindBodySpirit Festival. She was giving a speech called 'Connections with your spirit guides', which I absolutely adored. What I loved even more was coming back to the stall I had seen the drum at the night before, and finding another drum leaning against the chair. I just couldn't stop looking at it. It wasn't part of the display items, and the lady at the stall was unsure if it was for sale, so I left her my number in case it was.

And with that, I went to work, finished all my work calls, and finally submitted my written notice.

Dark nights and dark knights

The following night, I dreamed about the drum I fell in love with. In my dream, it was sold to another woman. I arrived just in time to make my counter-offer and it was accepted. I knew I had overpaid and that it wasn't worth that price, and found myself justifying my decision, arguing that healing myself and others would be worth the cost. Yet when I looked at the tool in my hands, my perception of it had changed: I still loved it, but the taste in my mouth was bittersweet.

When I woke up, I took out the Icaros I learned in Peru and practised them. Then, I sent an email to my boss asking for a reimbursement I was offered back in 2018. I knew it was a long shot given the time that had passed, but since it came to a month's salary, I just had to give it a try.

A few hours after I hit send on that email, it suddenly felt so simple, when just days before I was debating it back and forth. I realised yet again how any change or challenge seems so much less of a big deal once I've actually done it.

That realisation showed me how much bigger I made things out to be than they actually were, as well as what I loved about walking the spiritual path. Once you leaned in and learned to see how every challenge was there to help you grow and develop, and the beauty and benefit it brought, that new level of consciousness was pretty insane. Hard to put into words, even—especially when trying to explain it to someone who has never experienced it.

I returned to the MindBodySpirit Festival a few hours later to listen to my coach's second talk. Dan, the film director I met in Peru, messaged to remind me of the video he had taken of me in the red dress, just as I was about to walk in. I had bought the dress from one of the local tribeswomen the day before. Dan had felt called to make that video, he told me, and said that it would serve as a reminder of who I was about to become.

It was a beautiful video, and yet I felt a lot of resistance towards it. Today, I finally understood why: I didn't see myself in that same light. This wasn't me, and never would be—which made the timing of that message even more profound, since the topic of my coach's talk today was 'transitioning', in which she would speak about her journey from the traditional path of the corporate world to the unconventional path of greater alignment. It felt like the talk was targeted directly at me—like I was *meant* to be there, in that moment, for that exact reason.

That conviction was all the stronger considering that I hadn't planned on attending the event initially, as the energy at the festival had never truly resonated with me for some reason. That morning, however, I suddenly felt oddly drawn to it—as if I *needed* to hear about the journey my coach had undertaken, as I was about to embark on the one that lay ahead of me.

When I got home, I found a few messages on my phone from the shaman I sat with during my first ceremony. Unknowingly, I had disrespected his teacher's lineage by posting about my journey with Papa Guilberto in the group.

I could see my mistake and his perspective instantly, and couldn't help pushing back the tears. With everything else going on, it had all become too overwhelming. Maybe it was one of those 'dark nights' my coach had described during one of her previous talks, or maybe I was simply overloaded. I needed a walk in nature and to get away from it all.

The truth was, I felt vulnerable, more than I ever had before—and also much closer to defeat, even as I knew that the true battle hadn't even begun yet.

Had I bitten off more than I could chew?

Likely. But I didn't regret it, even though I felt like I was being tested to my limits. I was still defending my decision to my family, setting new boundaries with Dan, and being told by my rental agency that my bike and furniture couldn't stay in front of my apartment.

Living an authentic life was exhausting.

Where had I gone wrong?

With Dan, I should have been clearer. With my ex-husband, more direct.

I had *chosen* this path, and yet my mood was all over the place. Frustrated and annoyed, I paced up and down my living room, until I finally understood the real reason behind my irritation.

I had barely heard from Jimmy, and it was really hard to comprehend that reality after what I was shown in Peru—even though I knew I had to take it with a pinch of salt. Especially after Dan shared with me that this could have been shown to me so I would learn what is *not* good for me.

Was he right? Was Peru just an illusion of what I wanted it to be?

It didn't feel that way, but then again, I wouldn't want it to.

Was my mind playing tricks on me? Was the medicine?

It would have been a very cruel way to show me to let him go, I concluded, and put that thought aside.

Snakes and more snakes

The day after became a day of reflections. It was the morning after what I understood to be my dark night. Afterwards, I had to sit in 'that sucks', and truly accept it.

Yes, everything coming together like that really sucked. And yet, somehow, I felt newly regenerated, as if it was waiting for me to be released. Even if I didn't see it coming.

The following morning, my son and I went to a charity sporting event to support our local community—through *our* version of support, that is, with coffee and a sausage sizzle. Not everyone can be an athlete.

It was a beautiful day out. The sun was shining for a second day in a row, and it was warm and pleasant outside. Once the event was done, it was time for my son to head over to his friend's place for a playdate.

We were at the bus stop ready to go, when he received a message from his stepmum. Nina now solely communicated through my son.

She texted him to let him know that he needed his basketball today, but the text came when it was too late for us to turn around and still make it to his friend's house in time. Since she was the one organising the event while he was with me, I had been kept completely in the dark.

That was frustrating on its own, but even more so after they texted back and forth, and she asked him if I would be around when his dad came to drop off his ball. My blood boiled. I was surprised how easily I still got triggered.

I understood this could become the moment we would come face to face for the first time since our falling-out. My body was going through a rollercoaster of emotions. I started contemplating my answers in advance, judging what I was wearing, as well as my whole being—before I paused, saddened by the effect this had on me, when just a moment before I was so blissfully happy.

I asked for strength and courage, and was reminded of when I followed other people's dreams—how it felt like I'd accomplished something, yet that accomplishment was empty. It seemed meaningless. The success was only on paper. That's when I understood I had to find the strength within myself and stand behind the decisions I had taken.

Why were their opinions so important in the first place?

They weren't, I realised. Not this time.

Suddenly, I became very calm. I sent my son inside, and waited outside for Nina and my ex to arrive.

Ten minutes went by, with no sign of either of them. I then called my ex to find out where they were.

He was still at home after coming back from a run just moments earlier, and wouldn't be there for another thirty minutes, at the very least. By the sound of it, it was also just moments ago that he had learned of what just happened.

Beforehand, that would have triggered the hell out of me. I would have personalised it and been angry about it all day. *Not today.* Instead, I texted my son to let him know his dad would still be a while, went for a walk and enjoyed the sun on my face, and concluded my next stop for the day: the tattoo shop.

THE TATTOO shop was closed when I arrived. 'Opening hours from 12 p.m.', the sign read. It was just after eleven.

Standing in front of it, I suddenly became very nervous. This wasn't my first tattoo, and getting one was usually not a big deal, but *this* one had more meaning, and would define me more than any of the others did.

It was another 'souvenir' I had brought back from Peru. It came to me throughout my stay, each day adding another piece to it, until it was complete only a few days prior to my departure. It would be much bigger than the other tattoos I had, and on a place on my body I had never imagined getting a tattoo.

To kill time, I sat down at the nearby mall, ordered a coffee and started journaling about my day. When I got up to head back to the tattoo store, I noticed my bag pocket covered in ink. One of my pens had leaked, leaving big black stains all over my otherwise beautiful nude linen bag.

Cleaning it in the nearby toilet, it suddenly hit me: this was no coincidence.

I was booked in for a consultation at a tattoo store in Bondi the following day, but the store I was visiting today had caught my eye while I was on the bus with my son. When I say it 'caught my eye', I mean it literally pulled my head in its direction. *This* was the place I needed to get my tattoo, and the confirmation came covered in ink.

I went inside the parlour and told the receptionist what I was after. She introduced me to Sid, the tattoo artist, and I booked my appointment with him for the eighteenth of June. I walked out and cancelled my consultation in Bondi.

LATER THAT night I spoke to the shaman I sat with in my first ceremony back at home. I was struggling with my post-dieta integration, and asked him if he knew anybody who could help. When he offered to talk to me himself, I jumped at the opportunity.

He got me out of my head and back into my body, out of the external world and back deep within. I felt connected to my plant when I spoke to him, and honoured to be walking this earth with this new ally. I also understood that I needed to reduce distractions and spend more time in solitude again to build on the connection I had developed in Peru.

Speaking to him stopped the chaos within me and solidified what still felt so open—especially after listening to him talk about his first dieta experience, and then his second, which he did pretty much back to back.

Thirteen plants were now residing within him, which made me admire him even more. No wonder he was so good at what he did! I obviously had a lot to learn, and after speaking with the shaman, I couldn't wait to begin.

Change is brewing

I woke up in the middle of the night, my body shivering, resenting the hot water bottle I held to my tummy. I could feel that I was in a different frequency, and the shamans' energy was surrounding me.

I dreamed of New Year's Eve, telling myself to enjoy the fireworks, not knowing what was to come. People were handing out free stuff, which I told myself to take as I wouldn't have money going forward. It was *awakening*...

I dreamed of meeting my neighbour, and that his girlfriend finally understood it wasn't coming from me. She didn't go away in my dream, but observed all from up close.

At the New Year's Eve celebration, an argument broke out between the people I was with and the group next to us. I just wanted to hide.

Later, in my real life, I was getting my son ready for school, with the shaman's words still echoing in my ears. I was determined to build a relationship with my new ally, Noya Rao, so I asked it to guide me to what it wanted, and it led me back to bed to meditate, rather than out in nature like I had planned. I listened.

Two hours later, I was struggling to get out of bed. It was as if the weight of a tree was pinning me down, urging me to rest. I felt guilty for staying in bed this long, even though my normal workday had not yet begun, until I surrendered, realising for the first time how tired I was, and how much I had overdone things lately.

Once I finally managed to get myself out of bed and finish all of my work calls for the morning, I read a book called *Working with Nature*—specifically, a part that talked about a vision quest. It was the first time I had come across such a concept, and only then understood the journey one of my fellow medicine brothers had just embarked on. This wasn't for the faint-hearted: four days out in the wilderness with no food, water, sleeping bag or journal, just you and your thoughts until your visions arrived. *No thank you!*

A message from Pauline interrupted my thoughts. Pauline was a spiritual teacher, shaman and entrepreneur. Her name came through to me in the context of the person taking me to my next shamanic level, following Peru. I was surprised, to say the least: a friend of mine was obsessed with her, but since I never saw myself as either a spiritual teacher or entrepreneur, I never paid her much attention. Not even when my friend gifted me her book for my birthday.

Nevertheless, I reached out to her on social media, asking if this was something she offered. She soon replied with a number of offerings, and asked which resonated the most. I had no idea. How could I choose the right path not knowing what exactly I needed her support with? My download wasn't really that clear.

So, I posed that question back out to the universe and asked it for a clue. The reply came hours later, just as I returned home with my grocery bags:

She will prepare you for your vision quest.

I nearly dropped my bags. The thought of setting myself up in wilderness in total isolation for days, to obtain advice and protection from my guardian spirit, felt more than just daunting. Think *Survivor*, minus cameras or support crew. I don't watch *Survivor*, and also wouldn't sign up for it in a million years. Partly because I'm blind in darkness, afraid of everything that moves and far from an experienced camper, and partly because my guardian animal/totem is a *snake*—which I still may be deathly afraid of, despite his promise of protection.

I swallowed. *Hard.* I decided to let that realisation rest for a little while, arguing that preparation meant I still had time to get used to the idea. I agreed to come back to it when the time was right (which would be *never*).

Meanwhile, I booked a roundtable with Pauline scheduled for my last day at work and her October retreat, which had just had three additional slots open up after her next year's event was already sold out. Lucky draw? We shall see…

Rollercoaster rides and valuable lessons

The following morning, I started cleaning the house, when I found seven missed messages on my phone. The money I had sent for Maya, the little girl from Peru needing an operation, had reached its destination. On my phone, I found pictures of her mum taking her to the clinic, as well as a long message from the organiser expressing his gratitude and support. He promised to sing for me in ceremony while he was there, so I would find strength and courage to continue on my path.

I couldn't stop the tears welling up in my eyes when I read this, realising I had more support than I knew (or felt!) right at that moment. Especially since I was once again in a state of fear about what life after the corporate world would bring—which was ironic, considering how often people had told me how brave I was over these past few days alone.

I hope I haven't given the impression that this step had come easy to me. It really hadn't—I was as afraid as anyone when it came to these decisions, if not more. I just wasn't going to allow my fear to stop me any more.

Thinking of it, most of what I did was *ridden* with fear— the love letters I had sent before I set off for the jungle being a prime example. What people called courage, I called *faith*—faith in the path I had chosen, and the support I had received. And in the future I was planning to lead.

I switched off my phone and went for a walk, an offering of tobacco in hand, which I sprinkled wherever felt right. I was in the middle of depositing some next to a tree, when I got a download of an area about twenty minutes from where I was.

Surprised, I followed the guidance and made my way over. When I arrived, the pathway was closed. Big barricades were blocking the entry, red ribbons warning against trespassing. As I was ready to make my way back, I got another download. Mortified, I watched myself doing just that—trespassing. I saw myself climbing through the marked area and the ribbons, and continuing onto that path.

I took a few deep breaths and looked around. Then, I slowly climbed through the barricades, my heart beating fast. Nearly making it to the end of the closed section, jittery and uncomfortable, and just steps away from the next opening, I heard a male voice indicating tree-cutting was in progress.

I literally ran out of there, while debating all the way back whether that was the right thing to do, or if I should have just continued on my way as I was shown. My conclusion brought me back to my values, and I relaxed. I was happy to trust in my guidance, but this had been taking it too far. This was breaking and entering, which was not something I was prepared to do.

Once that thought had crystallised, it was quickly replaced by another: that today had taught me to listen to what I would and wouldn't do. Grateful for the experience, I laughed at the adventure, until the next realisation stopped me in my tracks:

Today you learned to set boundaries with your spirit team.

June

Winter had hit Sydney, and it was starting to show. The wind had picked up significantly, and it was freezing outside—by Sydney standards, at least, and also for anyone who had just returned from a crispy thirty-two degrees in the jungle.

That morning I met Lauren (the lady with the parking ticket), who took me to Palm Beach for a walk and, later, for lunch in Avalon. That walk was eye-opening, on many levels. We talked openly, allowing her to sit in her discomfort and release the pain she was feeling in her heart. There was a visible shift in her at the end of our catch-up, as she perked up considerably and was in very good spirits.

I shared my journey from Peru with her, as well as the oracle reading from the cacao ceremony. She then offered to come up with a program to teach me what she knew. For a moment, it felt like she had received a download with an inkling of how this would look like, and where she would go from there.

When we reached the café, I realised something else: I suddenly became very afraid of spending. It was time I got my finances in order, and fast.

Meanwhile, the lady I had met at the MindBodySpirit Festival reached out, apologising once again for not being able to sell the drum. She had decided to keep it, after an impromptu healing session by her stall led her to that conclusion. Instead, we explored the possibility of doing dieta together in September, and she offered to carpool with me—completely out of the blue. It made me think it was no coincidence that we had met.

She then told me about a drum-making class in October, and another retreat in July. When I opened her email moments later, goosebumps ran across my whole body.

A women's circle, scheduled the weekend after my last day at my work.

Was that why the 15th of July came through as my last day at work?

ON MY way back to Coogee, I stopped at my favourite coffee shop. While I had always been friendly with the owner, today was the first time we'd ever had a proper conversation. I told him about Peru, and how I had just quit my job. He told me about his journey building his business, at a time when it had seemed impossible.

It was both comforting and nourishing to hear his perspective, especially when he told me how he had moved from the dark side to the light, after realising the project he had been sent to South America for involved killing all local businesses for the farmers. Instead, he cut all ties with his former work and opened his own business, supporting local farmers in his own right and never casting a look back at what he had walked away from.

The icing on the cake came when he offered to let me work at his café any time—no commitment, as flexible as I needed it to be—if or when I was short of cash. I gave him the biggest hug before I left, and felt like I was floating all the way home. I had found once again that support was available wherever I went, and that I just needed to trust. Yes, it would come in different forms than it had in the past, but it was there nevertheless, guiding and supporting my journey throughout.

Back home, I had a full-on day at work, communicating to my partners and peers my decision to leave the company. It was bittersweet. Some of them reacted really beautifully, while many others took the news a lot harder than I imagined.

The most surprising part? Telling them about my decision yielded revelations about how many of *them* wished to do the same.

Riding the waves of change

I didn't have any particular plans outside of work the following day, and with my work schedule rather light after finishing late, I was looking forward to a slow morning and a sleep-in. That turned into an early-morning call with my rental agency to discuss my fire alarm check-up, and a cup of hot lemon.

I looked after my pets and cleaned the house, my mood judge-y and on edge. When Jimmy texted, highlighting with his message that he was still miles away from where I was, it was disappointing at first, but that feeling passed surprisingly quickly. My outlook on life had definitely changed in that department. Before, it would have absorbed me all day, would have been the *essence* of my day. Not any more.

I turned my attention inward, had a long hot shower, and really indulged in it. I thought about what I could reply, and decided to put it away and start my day with purpose instead, filling my life with light.

My mood shifted momentarily. I was taking my power back. Thinking about the upcoming weekend in July gave me something to look forward to. I was excited about the new friendships it would bring and the person I was becoming through this process, as well as the lessons I was learning along the way. Feeling optimistic, I decided to take my motorbike out for a spin.

Less than two hours later, I came home feeling defeated and deflated. Somebody had hit my bike, and done a runner. I had taken it to the petrol station next door to get my tyres pumped before the ride, when, just as I was about to leave, I noticed that my front brake had been bent in the opposite direction. When I took a closer look, I saw my back brake had been bent as well, and spotted scratches on my mirror. That's when it dawned on me what must have happened. My brakes bent, my foot stall misplaced, my mirror out of whack—I was looking at my new bike in sheer horror. At least I wasn't on it when it happened.

The thought of someone just hitting it and leaving it there like that made me very angry. The least they could have done was leave a note offering to pay for the damage, or an apology. They probably didn't do so for a good reason.

Understandably, the ride after that was far from enjoyable. With my broken brakes and leg stand, I felt anxious riding the bike, and found myself to be floppy and unfocused.

Was that where I was right now? Had I gone from on-purpose to indifferent?

It felt like a whirlwind of change at the minute, each new day another loop of the rollercoaster, and part of me wished I could just catapult myself back to the jungle and relive the experience I had just had—to remind myself of the journey I'd just been on, and why I signed up for what I did. It was time to dust off the journal from my travels and to walk down 'jungle memory lane'.

Once I finished my ride, I went to the police station and reported the incident (also not something I would have done in the past). The officer was nice, took down all my details, snapped pictures, and promised to ring around to see if anyone had seen or heard anything. He then asked me if I wanted to take that person to court.

'God no,' I replied, a little surprised. 'I just want my brakes fixed.'

On my way back I sent a message to my rental agency, telling them about the incident and requesting an exception to park my bike in front of the house again. I was proud of myself. This 'new' me was standing up for herself, and I liked it!

To celebrate, I decided to treat myself to a hat that had caught my eye as I walked to the station. When I tried it on, it fit like a glove.

My new hat on my head, I then sat outside my house on my outdoor furniture, enjoying the view as long as I could, knowing its days were numbered.

My neighbour joined me for a little. It was nice to be able to have a long, uninterrupted conversation and clear the air. He was surprised by the messages I had received from his now *ex*-girlfriend, and was transparent about what he had shared with her before. It also gave me a good opportunity to share more with him about Jimmy, whose sister had connected with me earlier that day.

When I got back to my desk, I took inventory of my day.

Had I done enough? Should I have been more productive?

When writing is your passion and your story part of that transition, it is difficult calling it 'work' at times. Maybe because, until now, work for me hadn't always equalled enjoyment, or at least not in the same way. All the things coming my way now felt exciting in comparison. Maybe that was why I struggled putting writing into the 'work' bucket. This was a passion of mine, something I allowed myself to do in between.

Could this really be the life I would be living going forward? *Could this truly become what I do day to day?*

The idea of it felt so foreign to me that I had to pinch myself to try to make myself believe it, while also cautioning myself that it wouldn't always come as easily as it had thus far. At times, it would require strength and dedication, finding the means to the end while embracing the challenge all the while. But, just for today, I allowed myself to leave this day behind with no regrets, and the hope that all would turn out as it must.

A few hours later I was chatting to a colleague, who had also become a dear friend. I wish I had recorded that conversation. What he shared was so beautiful and encouraging! The thing that stood out the most was when he told me how evident it was that I had cared about *everything* at work—the people, the business unit and the business overall—which, for many, sometimes got lost in the day to day. He also told me that not many people would have the courage to do what I was about to, and to go in with all my heart.

That gave me courage, strength and hope—hope that there were people supportive of my journey, and who wanted to see me succeed, *my way*. Even though 'my way' might be a little unconventional, arguably.

FINDING MY WHY

OW! I KEPT saying that word over and over again
that day—just *wow!*

My day didn't start that way, of course. On the
contrary, it had been fairly uneventful to begin with.
I had a quick catch-up with one of the medicine girls, talking
about life and how it had shaped us, before I went to Waver-
ton for a walk near Balls Head.

This was a place that was very holy to me, a little sanc-
tuary I always felt called to for matters of the heart. It first
called me a few years back, when my marriage broke down,
and then again when my granddad died. I spent nearly every
day there during that time.

It was also the place I truly came home to myself, for the
first time. Each day I walked there, and with every step I
took, I spoke to the trees there and heard them responding,
my creative brain activating as they spoke to my soul. When
I walked there today, another long poem emerged. It wasn't
quite ready yet, but the core of it had already soared.

On my way home, I texted Jimmy and he invited me to
dinner. That would have been enough to make my day, but
the true highlight was a catch-up with a colleague, who told
me how inspiring he found the step I was taking and how

many people feared saying 'no' to steady employment with a hefty pay cheque—him included. He agreed with me that there was more to life than a corporate role, and asked if he could follow my journey from a distance.

Now, I should add that this is someone I have always looked up to, and who held a much (much!) higher position than me, so hearing that from him just meant the world. Doing so, he told me, would encourage his own step one day, and help him find his happy place, too.

That phone call was all I needed to fill my cup up to the brim. Not only did it show me that I *was* on the right path, but also, once again, how many others wished to do the same! And with that, my path suddenly became even more important. It was no longer just my path I was walking—I needed to do this for others too, so that they could feel the same one day. Show them that it was possible to dream and to accomplish all they desired—and more!

That realisation suddenly gave my situation a lot more meaning and drive, and catapulted my ambition. It was something I could hold onto when the darker nights appeared, because a mission that isn't just your own is so much grander. It was one I *couldn't* abandon; it was like when I became a mother, and realised it was no longer about me any more, but all about the baby.

With that, a promise was born—to all who were with me during this time, watching me take this step, I promised not to surrender until I reached the point that they felt they could do so as well. I guess this is what Mark Twain meant when he said, 'There are two important days in your life—the day you are born, and the day you understand Why.'

Today, I finally understood *my* WHY.

Wow. Just wow!

Release and let go

The next day I spoke to a wellness coach who had reached out to me a few days earlier. She was keen for me to join her business, and since this was still within the wellness sector I agreed to jump on a call. For nearly fifty minutes I fired question after question at her. Not in a bad way, of course—they were all filled with genuine curiosity, but I wanted to truly understand what I would be signing up for, if I did.

She answered all of my questions patiently, and gave me a lot to think about. I then went for a walk, stopped by a bakery to get a hot chocolate, and found a new path to walk on. It was sunny outside (warmer than inside my house by a mile), and just the perfect day overall—except for the fact that I still hadn't heard from Jimmy. As much as I tried not thinking about it, it kept playing on my mind, making me question the promise and commitment I had given in Peru.

As I walked, another poem emerged, a butterfly danced beside me, and a dog came in for a cuddle. I sat by the ocean for a while, taking in all its beauty, filled with so much gratitude and admiration for where I lived. It was always beautiful here, but especially so when it was sunny. I felt content—in my being, in my doing. I even got dressed up that day, just for myself.

On the way back I bought myself the little throw-on I had spotted in a shop window the day before. It was half price, and just divine (especially at that price), but I still needed to give it some thought before taking the leap. I want to re-iterate here, I am not half as shallow as I may sound. For the longest period of time, I prioritised work and being a mother, and didn't pay enough attention to how I looked. So these moments actually became quite instrumental for me, because I was learning to treat myself better as a result.

Nevertheless, my brain fought me hard over it, as it did with all my spending in those days—even when it was still way within the daily budget. I could feel a fear of spending money developing ever since I resigned, but also a new appreciation and understanding that I *could* spend a lot less than I had done in the past. It would be harder during the weeks my son was with me, but I could budget for that as well.

I bought snacks and nibbles and headed home to get everything set up for an evening with my friends. When the girls arrived, we had dinner and made candles out of beeswax, setting an intention onto each one. One candle represented *release*, and the other *an invitation*.

The invitation intention came through to me almost immediately: *to connect with the chief's daughter, Noya Rao and the shaman within me.* However, my friend who was leading this activity asked us to start with the release.

As the other two started sharing, I started thinking about my own release. What did I want to let go of? Fear? Self-doubt? In one way or another, I needed both for my next journey.

When it was my turn to share, one of my friends got up and hugged the other. It was perfectly normal, and completely fine given the circumstances, but what showed up for me in that moment was *rejection*. I felt left out.

That's when I understood that this was what I needed to let go of: rejecting myself and *perceiving* rejection, so that I could allow love to enter.

I understood that rejection had kept me safe. It was uncomfortable, sure, but this was a discomfort I knew. This new way was asking me to open up to a new possibility: to be loved *fully*, *wholly*, *solely* and *entirely*.

It might be difficult to understand as an outsider looking in, observing my behaviour from a different angle, but the truth is that we are all mirrors. If it feels like a rejection to me, the question I need to ask myself is: *Where am I rejecting myself?*

The answer was: in many, many ways, since I was still healing the wound of not being good enough.

That's when the conversation took an unexpected turn and shifted to the time I was bulimic. I was barely fourteen when it began. My friend asked me what triggered it, and how I overcame it. The simple answer was that my mum caught me in the bathroom.

Another two memories popped into mind. Memories that in hindsight showed me how differently these events can be perceived. However, at my young age—and particularly in my weakened state—confirmed my self-talk about not being good enough. Because here's the thing with the stories we tell ourselves: once we convince ourselves of something, we take every opportunity to confirm it, until the story grows so big in our heads it becomes the only voice we listen to.

I lit both candles after the girls left. I was ready to release what no longer served me, to forgive what had to be forgiven, and to welcome all new connections coming my way.

Ignoring intuition

Quite timely following that release, my sister and I connected about a potential family getaway in December. This would be the first time we came together as a wider family since the borders closed due to Covid a few years ago. Excited, we started planning.

However, when the conversation shifted to my job, my guard came up—especially when my sister kept sharing her concerns, and asking questions I simply didn't have an answer for. So far, all I had to show for myself was the September dieta, the upcoming Ayurveda course, and the getaway retreat with Pauline to get me ready for my vision quest. How do you describe that as a 'plan' to family members?

I wanted to be understanding of her views, but I also didn't want to continue having to justify myself all the time. The question I'd been asked in Peru echoed in my ears:

'*Can you replace knowing with faith?*'

I could, when it was just about me. Add my family members to the mix, and it got a lot more complicated. Truth was, I didn't have a plan—not to the extent that I would normally have or would *want* to have a plan, to say the least. And that was scary. *Fucking* scary, to be precise. Even more so when I was challenged on it.

I knew I had a pending decision regarding the wellness opportunity, and needed to let the coach know what I was going to do one way or the other, but still I was hesitating. While I really liked the holistic approach, I wasn't so sure about the supplements that came with it.

At the same time, my friend Val reminded me of something interesting: she asked me why I couldn't go it alone as a wellness coach, after all the training I had done.

Could I?

Yes, it would make things easier to begin with, but I also wouldn't be backed up with science or have a nurse on standby, as I would if I went with the online platform I was considering using. On the other hand, I also wouldn't have to sell the supplements provided by that platform, which was a requirement but which I didn't fully believe in. That made the decision difficult, because to me, my reputation was more important than having my own business—being able to live in integrity and not put my name on the line for something I might end up regretting later. I had worked too hard and too long to build up that credibility to ruin it through network marketing.

So essentially, that meant I was leaning towards saying 'no'. So why was I hesitating? In hindsight it was probably driven by two factors: 1) The conversation with my sister and wanting to have a plan, and 2) The inability to move forward without one.

To be on the safe side, I asked for guidance on the decision: a red feather if I should go ahead with it, a blue one if I shouldn't. Leaning back, I took a deep breath and waited for the right moment to receive that guidance.

THE FOLLOWING day I went for breakfast with my bestie, and we had a lovely catch-up over Bircher and tea. As we were about to leave, I found a message on the basketball group chat that told me that my son was sick and would be unable to make it to that night's game. That was no problem on its own, of course—it just wasn't the way any mother would want to find out that her son is sick. I called him and offered to take him home earlier, but his wish was to stay where he was.

Luckily my friend was still there, who reminded me that he was just a little boy who was sick at home and wanted to stay where he was. That helped me step away from it somewhat.

Instead of being angry, I decided to get on with things. I booked the family vacation for December, and then said yes to the wellness opportunity. On that morning, it simply felt right—especially since it would allow me to share my learnings along the way. I figured that wherever it took me, I would learn from it one way or the other, and it prompted me to set up my own website and educate myself further. Plus, I could always make a final call further down the line if the concept didn't resonate, and the upfront investment of $165 seemed worth it if the opportunity taught me how to become my own boss (I made it as far as the set-up.).

I had also finally gotten on top of my finances. Ever since I'd created an Excel sheet with all my outgoing/incoming cash flow against my budget, I had gained significantly more confidence; I knew exactly where I was, and how I was tracking. The feeling was exhilarating, and I was surprising myself with just how quickly I was able to bounce back these days.

Something else triggered within me that day. Maybe it was because of what had just happened, because I knew my son would come home later that day, or just because of the journey I had been on lately, but for whatever reason, I reached out to my mother and thanked her for her support. I told her about my upcoming studies, and sent my sister a joke.

It felt good to be standing on my own. *Living in my being.* Whether it was the wellness website I had created on the side, or how natural it felt to now express myself fully, since it was everything I liked and was passionate about—it felt great!

There's a lot of power in living in one's truth. I highly recommend it.

A day of wins! (almost)

I went for a run today—no goal, no agenda and no pressure.

It was by far the best I've done in a while, both in speed and distance: seven kilometres in forty-five minutes, barefoot along the beach. It's crazy what flow can do for you! Especially considering that it was a last-minute decision I made after one of my girlfriends sent me a picture of her running on an empty beach. That was all it took to get me out of bed and into my trainers.

On the way there I pondered the power of our minds and of our belief systems, and how mine had recently been clouded by other people's worries, making me believe in their realities instead of mine. I had to stop doing that and trust in myself and my journey more, as well as in the guidance I was receiving. After all, being a super-manifestor went both ways: we attract what we send out. That was one big lesson for me this morning.

The other one came from talking to my son about his grandparents' concert at school, highlighting once more our disconnect on that subject. Both Nina and I wanted to attend the event—like we should, I figured, knowing the importance she played in his life.

What I didn't expect was to receive push-back. Push-back that first came disguised in the form of my plus one, and at the end with him not attending. And while that day initially felt like a win, it ended up becoming another lesson in just how far I was distancing myself from my boy at the time. It would take me another two years to get back on the same page with him and many, many conversations thereafter. But more on that later.

Later that night, I finally told my team at work that I was leaving. Saying goodbye to the people I'd worked with for so many years was the hardest conversation I'd had about this yet.

If you keep giving everything out for free, that's what people will think it's worth

For the past three nights in a row, I had been dreaming about the wellness business. Two nights guided me to go ahead with it, but in my waking hours I found myself still resisting it, looking for red flags in everything I saw. One could even go so far as to say that I was trying to find holes in the program for no apparent reason.

On the final night, I dreamed about being a healer—a good and humble one, and one who was about to enter into the world. It felt amazing when I woke up.

That changed four hours later, after I finally finished a seemingly endless virtual conference at work. My diary entry at the end of the night read:

'I am snappy, my mood crappy, don't know why, feel irritaty.'

The last part was a lame attempt at making a joke. Not a very good one, arguably, but at least my 'crappy' still has a sense of humour.

I tried tracing that feeling back to where it had begun. The coaching call I'd had earlier had gone really well, as did the time I'd spent with my son.

Was it the virtual conference? If anything, I would have expected that to confirm my decision.

I had also received a message from Dan, the film director, telling me that some personal advice I gave him had been spot on. So what was my problem?

There had been a moment in a coaching call I'd had with one of the associates when I felt I should be charging for my advice. What I was sharing had nothing to do with business and (as always) I was giving everything away for free. I had never monetised my knowledge, even though I had invested years in external coaching, signed up for multiple courses, and spent over twenty-five thousand dollars on my own growth and development over the past six years alone. And that was all outside of everything I had learned at work, and one of the reasons so many called me their mentor or coach or wanted to join my team.

But again, I had never monetised that. *Was that where my frustration was coming from?*

The moment I started exploring that feeling, my anger evaporated. I had crossed my own boundary. It was time to seize the rewards for the efforts I'd invested, and the time it had taken me to step into a new way of being. Was that where the coaching business would take me?

It was time to find out.

Finding stillness in an overthinking mind

The next morning I went for a long walk and immersed myself in nature. It was a perfect day! The beauty of these walks was that I always had insights, always felt in flow when I got back, and always found an answer to my challenges.

As usual, my mind went into overdrive for the first twenty minutes, my thoughts, that day, swirling back and forth between the man I was in love with, and where I was headed with work. Then, I finally surrendered and walked in unison with the trees.

I still found it fascinating how at peace I always felt when surrounded by nature—how still I felt inside, and how easily the wisdom of the trees entered my mind. That feeling cleared all my doubts almost instantly. And that day, it told me to trust in my journey, and where I was headed with Jimmy—my 'husband to be', if I could trust the vision I'd seen in Peru.

The even more surprising part was that I actually trusted their wisdom, knowing they knew things I didn't and believing in their experience over mine. After all, they had a few more centuries on their backs than I did.

On my way back I wrote a poem, and then a post in which I openly shared about my plant medicine journey, referencing the dieta I just had with my first tree. This showed me once more how much creativity resides in all of us if we can just find the mute button and cut out the outside noise once in a while, eliminating all distractions so that we can surrender and be at one with who we are.

I then made a plan to speak to the wellness coach the following day and officially kick-start the wellness business, as well as pay for the website in the meantime to lock in my commitment. If I had learned one thing about myself these past few weeks it was that I needed to lock things in quickly, or else they wouldn't happen.

There was a part of me that still couldn't believe that I was only four weeks away from ending my career in the corporate world—my *life* for the past decade and a bit, considering how much time I invested in it. To be 'out of a job', as many call it, and on a path to purpose. So many people I had spoken to over the past few weeks had called this step incredibly brave, but it was getting very real to me now. Very, *very* real, to be precise.

That's when I reminded myself that I was surrounded by people who had launched their own businesses, and that I should trust in the knowledge that had been shared with me in Peru. Either way, there was no going back now. The pressure was rising, and so was the twirling in my head.

TAKING MY
POWER BACK!

Y MORNING BEGAN with a conversation with the wellness coach, as I started figuring out the best way to get myself started in the business. I then received a call from Lauren, asking me for advice to get her Ayurvedic business off the ground.

I felt on fire! Right up until I saw my son panicking, caught in a crossfire between his stepmother and his friends. Since Nina and I were still not communicating, it complicated a lot of things, and seeing him on the receiving end was killing me. I wanted to fix things, for his sake.

Maybe this was meant to show me that it was time to address the inevitable, and that I was strong enough to face this head on. To ease his mind, I called his dad and clarified the situation within seconds.

When we set off to the city moments later, I earned a crooked look from him when I put on my new poncho.

His reaction did startle me for a quick second, but I felt good in my skin again the moment we started walking. While my poncho may not have been to his taste, I liked it and that was more important. (In the past I would have changed my outfit; not any more.)

With that hurdle overcome, we ended up having the best day! We strolled around the city, bought him a microphone for his YouTube channel, had velvet cake at our favourite bookstore, and met up with friends at Vivid a few hours later. When we got home, I finished my second poem of the day.

I felt strong—back in my power, and back in alignment with my flow. That could have had something to do with the dream I had the previous night that showed me a reunion with Jimmy was near, filling my heart up with joy.

Addressing the elephant in the room

After dropping my son off at the cinema to watch a movie with his friends the next day, I texted my ex-husband. What yesterday's situation with my son showed me was that I needed to address this head-on. So I reached out to his father, hoping he could support me on the way. Unfortunately, at the time, he wasn't able to assist me.

What this taught me, in hindsight, was to reflect on my actions leading up to that event. Words I had spoken, that no longer represented the truth. The fact was, Nina was— and is—playing a parental role, and it took writing this book to finally recognise her for what she is: a crucial figure in my son's life.

Letting go

I could feel that the people entering my life now were coming into it with a purpose. Like the friend of a friend from

Argentina, who reconnected with me out of the blue after many years and offered to take me back to the jungle. It was as if the universe was trying to show me that everything was prepared for my transition.

This made me examine the other relationships in my life, too, especially with one friend in particular. It was someone I used to be very close to, until the last time we spoke when I was in the final stages of my separation. I don't lean on my friends very often, but in that moment, I needed someone who would listen to me with an open heart and open mind, and tell me it was going to be okay. Instead, I found myself justifying my decision for the entirety of our conversation. (*There was a theme, there…*)

She had tried re-engaging with me on a couple of occasions, but the hurt was so deep that I never took her up on the offer. But today, I felt ready to move on—forgive what had to be forgiven, and finally let go of it all.

I reached out to her on social media and told her why I was no longer in touch, as well as what our conversation had meant to me back then. She didn't recall the conversation in great detail, nor that particular moment, but she also shared that she was going through a hard time at the point we spoke.

The funny thing about forgiveness is that when we're finally ready to take that step, the reaction of the other person becomes secondary. Because we are no longer doing it for them—or their apology—but for ourselves. And sometimes, just sometimes, it's exactly in these moments that we are reminded that everyone is dealing with their own load as well, and that they too are trying to do the best they can with what they have.

After clearing the air with her, I wrote a long post about it on social media, which triggered an ex-boyfriend of mine to respond. He asked if I was referring to him when I wrote this, and if I was still holding a grudge. If I was, he said, he thanked me for letting it go.

I could see how he could have interpreted it that way, considering we had just reconnected after bumping into each other in the street. But it meant a lot to me nonetheless, because it proved we never do these things intentionally, and that deep down inside we do care how we're perceived, whether we're conscious of it or not.

And with that, I could finally put that memory to bed—knowing that, above all, I had just needed to voice it for myself.

Speaking of what needed to be voiced, that night also triggered the message I had been avoiding all along: the one to my Jimmy.

As much as I loved Jimmy, I did not love his constant disappearances, and today I finally told him so. I stopped making excuses for it, or filing it under the promise I had made in Peru to be patient: I told him he could either be in my life or out of it, but he couldn't keep drifting in and out as he did.

At first, it felt *so* right to say that! *Strong and powerful.* Then, the fear kicked in, making me regret the harshness of my message, and question whether he really deserved the feelings I'd shared.

I re-read my message over and over again, until something fascinating happened: I found peace, knowing that wherever it went from here would be better than where we were right now. Maybe not straight away, and it may hurt for a little while, but where we were was not a long-term solution, and not how I had envisioned a relationship—of *any* kind, but especially with a partner. I wanted my partner to be there for me, to make me a priority, just like I would for him. Yes, there would be moments where work would take over, but that should be the exception, not the rule. And if that wasn't going to be my reality with Jimmy, then I no longer wanted the fantasy of it. I wanted the *real* thing, the real *everything*.

So, for better or worse, I concluded that I had made the right decision—for me, and maybe for *us* as well. Because the other thing I had learned about boundaries was that you also need to set them with people you want to *keep* in your life.

Connections

I went to the grandparents' school concert the next morning, ready to face Nina for the first time in months. I was unaccompanied, since, as luck would have it, neither of my girlfriends was available at that time.

I was pretty nervous when I left the house, but as I got closer to the venue I was reminded of my place in my son's life, and relaxed. I had *nothing to prove*. Squaring my shoulders, I went inside.

She wasn't there, and neither was my son.

I chatted to one of the other mothers, and looked at our kids' projects that had been put on display by the school, feeling immensely proud of what they had accomplished. The emphasis on sustainability, connections and mental wellbeing was very evident, and since those were all topics close to my heart I couldn't wait to talk to my son about it the next time I saw him.

When I got home a few hours later, I found a message on my phone from Jimmy. My heart cringed as I read it. It sounded like *defeat*.

He apologised for the delay in his responses, and told me that he was doing it to everyone right now. That made me genuinely sad: he was an incredibly hard worker and had been in a busy job for as long as I had known him, managing multiple demands simultaneously while distancing himself more and more from everything and everyone else. And yet I also needed him to see *what* he was doing—not just to me, but to himself, and others as well.

Later that night, I wrote a long post about connections, community, honesty and, most importantly, truth: how easy it was for us to find it, how quickly we could lose it as we aged, and how important it was for someone to remind us of it when we did, even if we didn't want to hear it at that time— or rather, *especially* when we don't want to hear it. And how, in order to get through to us, that person would sometimes need to risk the danger of not being liked. Because when you love somebody very deeply, more important than being liked by them is telling them what they need to hear, or else you end up watching them approach an iceberg, knowing they'll collide with it unless you raise your voice.

Trusting in the unknown

The next morning, over coffee and scones, my freshly renewed Argentinian friend told me about her career as a medicine woman as I listened intently. Her path had taken her all over the world, albeit in a different direction than the one I was choosing. Nevertheless, she was incredibly impressive, to say the least, and made me question my own path ever so slightly.

Later that night, I received a vision on that same topic. I was shown that she hadn't come into my life to *challenge* my path or change my course: on the contrary, she was there to confirm it.

In the meantime, I was challenged by friends and family to take the inner guidance I was receiving with a pinch of salt. (Wish I'd listened.) While I knew that this was likely a rather sensible perspective, at the time my heart couldn't help believing in what it saw with such conviction. Of course, I wanted to know *where* my path would lead me, but my commitment remained the same regardless, as did my trust in the belief that whatever was meant for me wouldn't pass me by and that things would have to start falling into place really soon.

In the meantime, I was going to practise the thing I hated the most: *patience.*

Six months down the line, I realised that this had been the hardest part of my journey—continuing to pick myself up and trust again, even though every time I came close to a win something would set me back. I would understand that this too was part of the journey I had chosen, and that building something from scratch took time, and a *lot* of practice. That transitioning from a past of achievement into an environment of rejections took time to get used to, but it would be those same rejections that would keep me going at the end—teaching me to grow, learn something new, and exploring other avenues and approaches.

I will fall down, and get up, more times than I can remember and will look back on this time with pride, knowing that I accomplished something pretty spectacular both *despite* it and as a *result* of it.

I will learn that climbing a high mountain just moments after standing at the peak of another, unafraid of starting all over again without a crew and a safety net, will take some real courage. As would believing in something different against all odds, and allowing myself to step outside the norm. That alone will be worth celebrating—*EVERY. SINGLE. DAY.* The rest is just a bonus.

Climbing up the mountain

My dreams turned very dark the following night. I wrote two pages on it in my journal in the morning, reviewing the week I'd had until then, and how it had somehow run away with me; how *I* had run away with it too, somehow. I needed to get back into being and back into presence.

As the words floated out of my mind and onto the pages, I became calmer on the inside, gaining perspective about the emotions I was feeling and the actions they caused—as well as the lessons they taught me.

I shifted my mind from doing what was 'right' (or 'wrong') to doing what felt *in alignment.* To follow my truth no matter what and act out of integrity in everything I did. While I had always operated this way to some degree, I now reached a new level of honesty I hadn't known before.

The truth was, I had lied to myself in the past, helping me mask the story I so wanted to believe in. This new version of me didn't allow for those excuses. And while it didn't always land well with those around me, I was learning that my responsibility, first and foremost, was to look after myself.

That then translated into saying the things that needed to be said (in the right way), and to no longer accept what I had in the past. I used to put people on a pedestal high above myself, admiring them and seeing them as whole, and myself as work in progress. That was a taught behaviour, of course, and a hard one to let go of. Seeing others as more worthy than you, and wanting them to like you so you feel like you belong, is where people-pleasing is born.

Well, *not any more!* Now, I would take a ladder and climb to that same height, ready to meet others eye to eye. I was no longer afraid of not being liked, even if that meant having to go our separate ways. It was on this day I stopped bending down and allowing others to walk all over me, rolling out the red carpet for them at my expense. *Enough was enough!* As my wonderful coach once asked me:

'How much longer do you want to keep suffering?'

The answer was: *No more!*

The suffering would end tonight.

Low blows reaching new levels

Later that day, I went to see my son at school.

In order to be in the right headspace, I went for a run first, wrote, and got some yummy food inside me. By the time I 'bumped into him' at the bus stop, I was in a great mood. That changed when he first didn't want to show me his school report, and especially when I found out I was blocked from his device.

The first part was easy to address, which brings me to my second point:

I knew deep inside my gut that something wasn't right. While my son has never been a great communicator over text, he had never totally ignored me for weeks on end. So, when I asked to see his phone and found myself on the blocked caller list, that feeling was confirmed.

I don't know if you've ever had to block anyone, but it actually takes quite a lot of steps to get there. There is no way to 'accidentally' block someone, as your phone asks you for several confirmations to ensure that this is truly what you want.

Finally, I asked him straight out: 'Did you do it?'

He said he hadn't.

Once he was on the bus, I messaged my ex-husband. 'Any ideas how I got blocked from our son's phone?'

Opening Pandora's box

The neighbours above me were moving into a house on the Central Coast. I knew this because they had knocked on my door late at night, asking me to move my motorbike so that the movers had easier access to their property in the morning.

Since the movers would arrive at 6 a.m., if I waited until then to move the bike I would have little window for sleep after finishing my night calls. So, good neighbour that I am, I went outside just before midnight, moved my bike to a different spot, and got back just in time before my last work call—not realising until hours later that I had dropped my phone along the way.

By the time I found it, it was complete toast. It looked as if half of Sydney had decided to drive over it in the last half hour. *Digital detox*, I tried to comfort myself through gritted teeth, as I stuffed it in my bag.

The following morning I was less compassionate about my neighbours' moving needs, as I was woken up before seven o'clock by the movers.

In my dream, a different tattoo artist was preparing to get to work on me in a theatre—the kind of theatre you find in a hospital, not one where you watch a show. I was nervous, to say the least. Especially since, in the real world, the draft I was sent by the actual artist just before my phone broke was different from what I had imagined, leading to seven last-minute messages with examples of what I was looking for before I finally warmed up to his original draft. One message later, and I called it a day.

What a mess!

Disconnected from technology (and, arguably, the world!), all I could do was surrender to trust as I made my way over to the tattoo shop that morning.

My son texted me that night, apologising for blocking my number.

I told him he didn't need to apologise. He told me he hadn't done it, and I believed him. I told his father the same. Blocking me was just not his style.

You could argue that a mother will always protect her son, but for the time being, that's where I had to leave it.

For now, I had to get my phone fixed, and get myself ready for the tattoo appointment.

It was time to level up to badass.

Signs

It was no coincidence that the tattoo studio was located where it was. As I walked through the city that day, I came back into the present moment with every step.

For the first time in a long while, I truly saw the city, and its people. The homelessness in that part of Sydney was insane, and so were the number of people high before eleven o'clock. That put my job decision into perspective—just like my India trip had done right after my marriage ended, when I had a mere hundred and thirty-five dollars to my name. It opened my eyes to how minor my problems were in the grand scheme of things. Then, too, the universe had looked after me, and then too I realised how much richer I was than I had ever known.

So, to the question I had pulled from the soul seeker deck yesterday that had asked me if I 'had enough', my answer today was one big fat *YES!* I had all I needed. *More* than I needed: I had a home, food, shelter, but more importantly, I had *choice*—choice to continue on the path I was on, or to pursue the life I *wanted* to live.

With that thought in mind, I sat down in the tattoo studio, surprisingly calm. And then, I got another surprise: the artist had included all of my asks from late last night, and absolutely nailed it! He asked me to take a good look at it this morning, to make sure I was one hundred per cent satisfied before he put it onto my body. It made me feel safe.

Fifteen minutes later, though, when he returned from the printer with the final print, my nerves kicked into gear. *Was*

I really doing this? Yes—apparently, I was. There was no turning back now.

Doors closing/others opening

My phone was truly beyond repair: it didn't just look like dust, it pretty much *was* dust. After being turned away from the second phone repair shop I'd tried, I succumbed to my new faith and got myself a replacement phone.

As I set it up later that night, I realised that I had lost not only the majority of my contacts, but also a lot of the pictures I had taken over the last few weeks. I could still retrieve some of them through friends and family, but the majority of them were totally gone.

I pondered the situation. On the one hand, this symbolised a pretty clear break from my old life—a very tangible one, marking the beginning of a new path and what was about to come. I could sign up for that—after all, whoever wanted to stay in touch with me after I left the corporate world would probably find a way to do so after I handed my sim card in at work.

But there was one person who mattered to me more than the others—Jimmy. His name swirled inside my head for the rest of the day.

Was this a sign that I had to let go of him too?

I rejected every other possibility.

Later that night, I reached out to my ex-husband, agreeing to let him take my son to the basketball game, knowing this would be the first time I would face Nina.

With that, I went back to work, finalising my last risk mitigation meeting with my boss before calling it a day just after midnight. One thing I wouldn't miss in future, for sure, were those late-night calls—not to mention those retention meetings.

How much was too much?

I got two good lessons in boundary-setting the next morning.

The first came in the form of a message from the mother of Maya, the little girl in Peru who I had agreed to support. She told me that Maya had been readmitted to hospital after the treatment I had paid for showed additional complications. She attached a picture of Maya, who looked as if she were in pure agony.

Her mother was asking me to send the same amount of money once again, to cover the additional costs—an amount that had been substantial enough when I sent it the first time, and was even more so now that I didn't have a job.

I thought of Tony Robbins, and how he had gracefully given away the last of his money to pay for lunch for somebody else. But the way her messages read made me feel *obliged* to do that. Sure, I *could* find another way to get by somehow, but there was something in my gut stopping me from doing so—a feeling I couldn't yet explain. It didn't *feel* right, when helping usually always felt right.

I sat with it and journaled on it, trying to understand what was happening right now and why. For context, what she was asking for was more than a month's rent in Sydney, which was a luxury I did not possess any more. But it made me feel bad trying to justify why I couldn't come up with the money.

I stepped back to analyse the situation. I realised that I had helped when I could, by offering to pay for her treatment myself when a fundraiser was the better answer. But my situation had now changed, and so too had my circumstances.

I wasn't responsible for saving everyone, as much as I was determined to move into the healing space. I needed to learn that my help had to come in different ways in future. In the past, I had always associated it with money; in the future, my currency had to be something else: time, healing, support.

It wouldn't be what the mother would want to hear right now, but I also needed to look after myself, and I had my boy to think of. I thought of Oprah, who had once mentioned in an interview a time when she kept being asked for money, and had felt bad for not supporting everyone who came knocking on her door. I finally truly understood that statement. And no, I am not comparing myself to Oprah here.

Don't get me wrong, I didn't blame Maya's mother: she was simply trying to find a solution for her child, and I was the fastest avenue. The pressure I felt was coming from myself.

So, I told her my limits, and reached out to the organiser of the Peru trip to kick-start the fundraiser.

Wind in my sails

Ever been strapped onto a slingshot and catapulted into the air? That's how today felt for me.

I woke up from the weirdest dream about the upcoming basketball dinner. My role in the dream was very clear: I had the upper hand over Nina, and could see her frustration growing about not being on top of things.

When I woke up from that dream, it took a moment to collect myself.

It didn't feel *right*.

It didn't feel *good*.

I didn't feel good.

Half an hour later, I sent my son off to school. As always, I ran to the window to continue our goodbyes. I pretty much belt them out of the window as he rolls his eyes at me, but I know he secretly loves it.

How do I know? Because the one day I didn't, I heard him shouting, 'You won't catch me!' and caught a glimpse of him racing down the stairs. He was *waiting* for me to do it. That's when I knew we had *a thing*—a ritual he'll remember me by when he grows older: the way I would always send him off in the morning, even when he was in high school.

Once he was gone, I tried logging onto my computer, but my technology wouldn't have it. Even connecting with the IT team was impossible that day.

I saw this as a sign, and changed my game plan. So, I proceeded to:

- Start my 30-day self-care challenge
- Post about it on social media
- Connect with the wellness coach about the business
- Get some new herbs to continue my 'witchery'

When I got home, my laptop was finally working—just in time to find a message from the manager running our India division, telling me she had taken a turn for the worse and wasn't able to come to work that day, or even update the slides for the operations review later that afternoon. I jumped onto it, prepared the slides on her behalf, and presented them later that afternoon, before reconnecting with work to see what I had missed in the meantime.

As the day progressed, I felt rather hopeful—about both the transition I was making, and my situation with Jimmy. We had made a lot of progress since my last message, and I could sense the journey coming to an end.

At the end of the day, I found myself excited and eager, and ready to take off the second skin from my tattoo. My excitement rising, I felt like a five-year-old before Christmas as I slowly peeled back the layers. 'Are we there yet???'

WITH THE last 'Bye, bye, bye, bye, bye,' my son raced out of the door like he usually did, and I was left to my own devices. Gosh, I *loved* having him here.

Today would be the last presentation I would ever give at work: operations review number sixty-five, to be precise (I counted). It would be the last time I had an opportunity to impact the business and balance the focus between people and performance. I wasn't ready for it, and I knew I was putting it off.

Why was I resisting it?

1 Because it meant looking at business for the last time.
2 Because it meant accepting that my journey in that world was coming to an end.

It's funny how we start truly appreciating something when it's time to let it go, and how it changes the conversations we have with people and what we tell them. These past few weeks have been humbling and saddening at the same time. I had been told by so many about the impact I was having at work that part of me wished there was a better system in place for people to share. And also that whoever is reading this right now picks up the phone to tell somebody who had a positive impact on them about what they did, and that it mattered.

After all, isn't that what life is all about? Knowing that, in doing our job as well as we can, we somehow made a difference to someone's life? That we weren't just sitting in our cubicles, or serving coffee, or driving someone to their destination, but were responsible for their smile that day, or whatever it was that helped keep them going? Maybe we gave them hope, or even just distracted them from whatever else was going on in their life.

What if we looked at every conversation that way?
Every person who was standing next to us on the platform?
What would we say?

I remembered the bus ride I had been on just a few weeks back. The driver was beeping at a man crossing the street on a red light as we were approaching. A businessman, I should clarify, who turned around and, swearing, flipped the driver the finger. Multiple times.

I thought about the bus driver first, how he didn't deserve that reaction, and I wondered how often he got exposed to something like that. Then, my attention shifted to the man. What triggered that reaction?

Maybe the bus driver had been the final straw for him, and his reaction a response to something that had happened that morning, that week, maybe even that year. That doesn't justify his behaviour, of course, but considering these possibilities can help us see the person in a different light. How often do we snap when, had we not been in pure coping mode, we would have reacted very differently? How often do we regret such behaviour the second we calm down?

The more people I meet, the more I realise that everyone is just getting along as best they can—some of us barely surviving, a few of us truly thriving. That's why we cling onto anyone who dares to do what they dream of, and look inside the little black screen to find the life we wish we could lead.

But what if, instead, we turned our attention inward? Asked ourselves what we could do today to move us closer to that goal?

Who would we need to call?

Who should we set a new boundary with?

Who would we let go of?

What would we let go?

What if we only needed one minute of courage to set us on the track we had always wanted to be on? Took that trip we always wanted? Left the relationship we knew was no longer good? What if we finally made the move and told someone we liked them?

How would our lives change?

How would yours?

DRAWING A LINE

ESTERDAY WAS full on. The presentation went well and brought many reflections, especially after I messaged with a colleague the next day, who told me the impact it had on her. She told me she always admired how hard I fought for my people and made the best out of every situation, staying positive in the most difficult times.

That message hit me deeply—more so than all the others had—because it summarised everything I believed about true leadership. It was her truth, and mine—yet seeing it right before you, written out in black and white, was quite fascinating. It let you know that others saw it too, and that my battles hadn't gone unnoticed after all. On the contrary, it had encouraged others to do the same.

I then went out for a walk and wrote a poem while resting by the shoreline. Those reviews always finished extremely late (even for my standards), and made me appreciate moments of rest even more, when I got the chance to take them.

I texted my neighbour to see how he was doing after the big party he had thrown last night. Instead of him, I got a message back from Emily:

'His head is fine, stay in your own business.'

And she's back! My reply was two laughing emojis, acknowledging that clearly nothing has changed.

But it had. *I* had changed.

Maybe it was the conversation I'd had with a friend the day before, who wasn't in a good place after her recent break-up. In her anger and pain, she used her energy to poke holes in pretty much everything I said.

This time, though, I was able to take a step back to not only recognise that this was coming from a place of hurt, but also understand that I didn't have to simply accept it. I then calmly expressed my truth. My reality was different from hers, and that was *okay*. It was okay to disagree, okay to not be on the same path, and okay to not be friends with everyone. At least that way you will gain your own respect, if not theirs.

In the meantime, what had really started playing on my mind was the prospect of actually publishing this book, and the reaction it will cause—not *just* for me, but *also* for me. That's a level of self-acceptance I will still need to learn. Because *if* this lands the way I am predicting it will land, a *lot* of people will not be pleased with me. And that's a reality I need to get ready for.

Lessons

I journaled two pages today, the second I woke up and without checking my phone first. It's fascinating to see what comes out when you allow yourself to just brain-dump everything that's on your mind. And it's even more fascinating to see what your mind feels like once you've got all that out: like an overgrown pond that had finally been cleared of algae, there was now room for flowers to blossom, and for new life to appear. But as long as it remains cloudy, so will be all the important stuff on your mind.

The good news is that there's a quick fix for that once you become conscious of it. Yes, it requires work, but more important is that it requires you to come to that decision.

Once I was finished, I spoke to a colleague who told me the story of when he wanted to relocate to Europe. His boss said *no*, telling him there were no opportunities. (His boss's boss, I should clarify.) He then asked the big boss if he could relocate to Dubai instead; again, the answer was *no*, there weren't any opportunities.

So, my colleague went home that night, searched the company's intranet, found a different department that had an opening, and applied. Not only did he end up getting the role, he also later changed his position and landed the role he originally wanted (in Dubai), and has since been promoted twice.

The moral of the story? Don't take no for an answer, and get your butt into action. The universe will challenge you, test you to see if you're up for the challenge. But when you do, it will support you, and teach you all you ever needed to learn.

My lesson in this came that same night. I was shown what was about to come to me through the lens of my best friend, who asked me to reconsider my decision about work.

She warned me of the perception it would have in the outside world.

The truth was, many people still considered the medicine to be a drug. The difference was that I had experienced the medicine and knew its power firsthand. The drink was so disgusting that you didn't drink it for pleasure, and the experience wasn't all love and glory, so you wouldn't come back just to chase the high. The medicine gave you a *lot* to work with (and through), and the thought of purging all night (especially in both ways) wasn't exactly enticing, either.

Added to that was the requirement to fast for several hours, and to say 'no' to most things we enjoy (coffee, salt, sugar, oils, etc.) for the week leading up to the retreat. So it's fair to say that the medicine required some serious commitment—especially since you went into it knowing that you might be met on the other side with pain just as much as joy, and would have lessons shoved in your face so frankly that there was no mistaking why you were there.

But along with all that, you also got to *release*! You got to let go of so many things that your body had been holding onto for decades, and free yourself from negativities, hate and self-loathing. It taught you how to love yourself in every form, and showed you where you had gone wrong, what your highest self looked like, and your potential, and taught you how to love unconditionally. At least that's what she had done for me, on top of teaching me to see those around me for who they truly are. *And myself.*

The effect didn't last forever, of course: after a while, your mind and emotions tried to push their way back in again. But it was still effective nevertheless, since it showed you the root causes of your hang-ups, your patterns and your possibilities. It asked you to reconsider how you had acted, and put a big mirror up in front of you so you could see it for yourself. Unlike the pond, it became a *true* reflection of who you were, what you had done to become that way, and how you could free yourself to become a better human. It gave me hope in moments I didn't have any, and a new beginning if I should choose to accept it.

That again required only one thing—*action* on my behalf.

Wounds in disguise

I needed hugs, people and love, I realised when I found myself more antsy than usual the following morning, having been triggered by something that would usually have left me cold. I journaled on it fiercely, trying to clear my mind, determined to be able to enjoy the rest of the day and see beauty where I currently didn't. I then asked for help and started on my gratitude list—the fastest way to change your state of mind apparently.

Then, it hit me! My family hadn't checked in with me since expressing their concern. That was where my anger was originating from— it confirmed an old story of mine.

I circled those words in my journal. It was a childhood wound that needed to be released before it started hurting the people I cared about.

As soon as I'd realised that a poem came through.

Embracing my uniqueness

I had developed a new level of honesty that scared me, and I hoped that I was communicating it in the right way. I shared with my mother the way I perceived my childhood. It was a hard poem to receive.

Jimmy came back to mind. (Blinded by my illusion, I still kept marching on.) I knew a relationship with Jimmy wouldn't be easy, that there were a lot of things he and I still needed to work through, and that it took time to move past these same moments.

What I needed to learn (among other things) was to live within the silence between my words. To give people time to take them in and respond in their own way, as well as allowing them to choose where they wanted to take it from there.

I understood that I had craved the feeling of being liked so much that disconnecting from it felt disorientating, but also grounding in a strange way. And while I was still nervous at times about how my honesty would land with others, I no longer questioned it and didn't regret expressing it, even hours later. Because it was honest. My truth. And that's how I had chosen to live life going forward.

Hugs, people and love

Ask, and you shall receive! This week I was meeting my bestie for lunch, a friend from Byron for dinner, and someone I met through the spiritual accelerator group for a walk by the beach.

For the meet-up with my bestie, I booked lunch at a cute little place in Neutral Bay. I was excited, ready to get a lot of hugs to fill my cup again, and realising more and more how much I needed people—*my* kind of people—as well as a loving support network. That made everything else a *lot* easier.

Dan had left me a voicemail, counting down the days until I moved into a life of transformation. He said it so beautifully, and with so much excitement in his voice, that it made me excited about it too, and showed me the difference between the way *he* was looking at it and where *my* head was going. I guess it was easier to look at it that way when you weren't directly impacted.

It reminded me of how I looked at Peru: how panicked I was at first, not allowing myself to look forward to the experience until I was nearly boarding the last plane.

Was I doing the same again?

Was the best part of my life around the corner, and I was just too afraid to believe it?

What if it turned out better than I ever imagined?

Speaking my truth

I woke up to a message from my neighbour's ex-girlfriend:

'Yes, go ask him to fix your windows again :D'

My blood boiled. Do people just wake up and decide to be nasty? Hurt people do, I guess.

I rewrote my first reply three times. As tempting as it was to step into that ring again and fire back, it was hardly productive.

Once I calmed down, I kept my reply simple:

'I didn't, he offered'

As soon as I hit send, though, I knew I couldn't leave it there. As I was typing the next part, her answer came through:

':D look, Tom deleted conversations with you back then obviously for a reason. And when I ask him he always says it is you who wants to get closer to him and you find excuses. He even show me your messages trying to give him advice about relationship and business (before doing that you should fix your own life first haha)
'You are not guru because you had time in Peru. Sorry :('

I heard myself saying to her that, if I wanted to break up their relationship, it wouldn't take much. All I would have to do was show him her messages, and that instead of blaming me she should try working on her relationship problems... Might have a better outcome.

Afterwards I added the following part:

'Instead, your strategy is to offend me. When I wanted to support you the day you showed up at my house, I offered to walk with

you and talk this out. I agreed to meet the three of us. I even met your dad, for God sakes.

'When we talked, you showed zero interest in me. And then you set up this petty chat "Coogee friends" to monitor your boyfriend's friendships.

'I told you, I'm not interested in him and yet you keep insulting me.

'I tried seeing it with humour, thinking it will pass and that you will see how ridiculous it is. Clearly not. I will not just sit here and let you waltz all over me, when I haven't done anything wrong. I told Tom I'm not interested. Told him that you seem to have that impression, and just so I am clear, friendship is all there is. So, stop blaming me for something that's broken on your side and go fix that. If that's the relationship you even want'

Her reply came two minutes later:

'Is not your fault I know. I'm not trying to put blame but it doesn't help the things he says to me. That's all. Have to go to work now have a good day

'I will not text you again don't worry'

I showered and thought about what just happened—wondering if her reply was sincere, or if she was recognising that I had leverage. I thought about my own steps these past few months. Had I done the same to Nina? Was *that* how it had felt to her? I too had my many reasons of course, and still believed she had gone way too far, but was this the state I was in before? Was *that* how Mum would perceive my poem?

The last thing I wanted to do was spread more hurt or cause any additional suffering—and I definitely saw myself as anything but a guru. Because the one point that Emily was actually right about was that I needed to figure my own life out first—and there was plenty of work for me to do there, especially now.

I left Mum a long voicemail, giving her context about where the poem originated from, why I had sent it to her, and its intent. I then added more context around my actual childhood wound.

It felt big for me to share this. The beauty of it was that it came with no expectations.

Meeting the girls that afternoon gave me great comfort—not only because it seemed to be a messy time for all three of us, but also because I realised how insanely liberating it was to share these moments with those you care about, and who care about you. How that changed the way you felt within seconds.

When I got back, I had a very open conversation with my boss. Turns out she too had wanted to do something different in the past.

Celebrating life!

My bestie was going on holiday with her new boyfriend. It was her first holiday away since separating from her ex-husband, and was thus a *very* big deal.

To celebrate, we decided to grab lunch at a new vegetarian restaurant in Bondi. The food was divine, and the afternoon was filled with a lot of laughter, especially after I handed her a going-away present: a pregnancy test, condoms, and the morning-after pill.

We laughed over 'wontons without meat' and 'fish that wasn't fish' as I told her about my experience getting the morning-after pill for her. I had to answer several questions on a form, learning that I am currently ovulating. But the best part came when the store assistant started entering my answers into the system. Since it was a 'fun' gift, I hadn't really given it much thought and ticked the first boxes available on the form—not thinking of the impression it would leave when I had to 'explain myself' to the store assistant. 'Thirty-eight years old, no condom'—oh dear! Her face literally said it all—as did mine, I'm sure! The things you do for your bestie...

I then wrote my second poem in German, and got some advice for the meeting I was having with the founder of a mental health company to talk about launching a technology idea I had a while back that would impact the way we teach our children and bring out the best in them.

Maybe it was healing my inner child that had made the difference, or speaking my truth in moments that mattered. Either way, those moments didn't add up any more! I felt calm and peaceful in my body (and mind), and like life was finally back on track again.

The highlight of that day was when I accidentally called my last day at work 'my birthday'. It just slipped out as we were waiting for the bill to arrive, and somehow felt so right. It was hard to explain, and yet it felt like just that:

The day I was reborn.

Head vs heart—which would you choose?

It was the last day of June, marking the end of the first half of the year and the beginning of the next. I took a moment to reflect on what had happened:

- Quit my job
- Gone to Peru
- Set a *lot* of new boundaries

- Closed doors
- Opened doors
- Wrote more than I ever had before
- Started doing yoga again
- Hula-hooped through the rollercoasters of life

Turns out my coach was right: after doing plant medicine, you didn't shy away from addressing your emotions any more. I had stopped judging them, or pushing them aside; instead, I now acknowledged them as they came, and allowed them to move through me as they needed to. Because I had learned that the worst thing you can do by far is push those emotions aside, or keep yourself so busy that you miss what's right in front of you.

Later that afternoon I caught up with Danny, a friend I had made at a recent coaching retreat. After listening to her journey intently, I shared a little about mine.

Danny had just met another woman who was in the role she had always wanted to have. Her eyes shining, she told me about the full-body experience she went through when she learned that this role existed. But, even though she had been about to speak to her boss about her future employment just moments after that, something had held her back from taking the leap. It was interesting, considering that everything in her body was screaming at her to take that opportunity—and then even more so when her boss moved their appointment at the last minute (like he always did, she added).

I wanted to tell her to be brave, to go for the opportunity and lean in all the way. But that was dangerous advice coming from someone who wasn't one hundred per cent there yet themselves—especially given how long it had taken me just to get to this point in the first place. And yet, secretly, I was waiting and hoping for her to text me later that afternoon to tell me that she had done it. She didn't.

It made me reflect on how many chances we didn't take, and how often I had had an opportunity that I didn't take advantage of. I knew that not visiting Peru the first time around was definitely one of them—but how many more of those moments were there in my past? How different would my life be now if I had said 'yes' to all those opportunities without hesitation? Who would I be today—and where?

I guess it doesn't make much sense to obsess over what could have been, and instead look at what's ahead. What opportunity lies in the path before you? And when it comes along, will you be brave enough to take it?

July

Finally, June was coming to an end. I had put way too much hope into that one month alone, and was so ready for a new beginning.

When it arrived, July greeted us with a forecast of eight consistent days of rain. Yet even that I didn't mind.

I pulled two tarot cards that morning—one showing me the cycle of life, and the other the support I had around me. The first card seemed to tell me that the cycle I was in was coming to an end, while the second asked me to trust in what was happening around me, and to know that I was guided throughout it all.

It also told me to rest and listen to my dreams, and to see the wonders I can find within them.

Meanwhile, in the real world, my neighbour asked me to help him move a table, and invited me for dinner and a drink after we were done. I hesitated, even though I really needed a relaxed evening with a friend.

'Sure Emily will be cool with it?' I asked. He told me they were done.

I couldn't have told him I was sorry, even if I tried. Because truthfully, I wasn't.

'Are you okay?' I asked instead. He seemed to be.

So, I said yes to dinner and a drink.

I decided that that night I would allow myself to let my hair down and cut loose from everything else—to release everything I was holding on to and just have fun, for the first time in what feels like a very long time.

Two hours later dinner got cancelled.

So instead, even though it was much less fun, I finished another sequence of yoga. As I was head down in my first pose, I could feel my perspective shifting, and once again I freed myself from the chains that I had shackled myself to. Nobody had asked me to become a nun in Peru, after all, to stop all male interactions and stop enjoying life. Just like no one had told me to address everything head on and fight for what I believed in. *That was my choice.* The control I imposed upon myself when everything else felt out of whack.

Yet the funny part was, this should have been the time when I was enjoying myself the most.

I still had a salary, for another month at least. *And yet I already acted like I didn't.*

I was still single, and the marriage I had been shown in Peru was not yet in sight. *And yet I already acted like I wasn't.*

I still needed my family. *And yet I was pushing them away.*

It was then I realised that I was boxing myself in, when no one else was doing so or had asked me to.

So, the next question was born:

What if I allowed myself everything I wanted? What would I do?

Two hours later, I signed up to give a TED Talk—on the topic of freedom.

Wish me luck!

Going for what I want

Jimmy circled through my head again all morning—first as I was getting dressed, and again when I was putting on my makeup. I *knew* I was going to see him today, even though we had nothing arranged. It was a feeling I had woken up with that morning.

That was followed by the crazy idea I should just show up at his workplace. I dismissed the thought momentarily, but it kept nagging at me, until it began to feel both ridiculous and right at the same time.

Was I really doing this? He might not even be in, my brain tried to argue. He might not want to see me, or might not have time.

I might embarrass myself. But I will finally know the outcome. I will have my answer. I nodded slowly.

(Anybody else playing ping-pong in their head, or is it just me?)

It felt insane! So much so that I wanted to puke at the thought alone.

On the bus, I nearly did. I was going to meet my girlfriend, and still hours away from when I would actually see him—if I actually did.

My friend was running late from her doctor's appointment, so I grabbed a sushi roll and sat down on a bench to wait for her. That's where I changed my mind again.

After all, this was stupid, my mind now told me.

What would I say? How would he respond?

But I already knew I *had* to do it. Needed to believe in myself and trust that this was the right next step ahead of me. I had dreamed of him for three nights in a row leading up to that moment, always in a different context, but always with him in spirit. But I was also afraid that he would shoo me away (figuratively speaking).

What if he doesn't want me?

He wants you, came back the reply. He too is just afraid.

In hindsight, I see how ridiculous this was, but in that moment I needed that validation to hit me with a sledge-hammer, by the looks of it. Now back to the story...

So, what could possibly go wrong?

A *lot*. A lot could go wrong, my fearful brain started to argue, every scenario playing out in my mind's eye as I sat on the train heading his way a few hours later.

What was I thinking? What was I going to say? 'How are you?'

Maybe I wouldn't even get to say anything. Maybe he wasn't even there.

OMG—*what if he IS there?*

I didn't know which scenario I was more afraid of. No, actually, I *did* know—the latter.

I had no plan, didn't know what I needed to tell him, and was basically just showing up at his workplace unannounced. It was my work situation all over again: *no plan apart from the plan to do it.* And then what?

Two more stops remaining—*I think I'm gonna puke!*

IT TOOK all my courage, as well as several deep breaths, to walk inside the kitchen at his work.

'Is Jimmy in?' I asked his co-worker, already hearing his voice out the back.

He smiled when he saw me, surprise written all over his face as he walked around the kitchen counter to greet me. I couldn't believe the effect he still had on me. After all, it had been two years! *How was I still so nervous around him?*

I had never felt anything like this before, at least not in the same way. In the past, when someone was gone, they were gone, and a couple of weeks down the line I was back on my feet. Sometimes it would even take me time to get used to them, when they were just away on a trip visiting their families, or returned from an overseas trip after a few weeks of being away. With Jimmy, everything was different—it was as if time stood still from the moment my heart opened wide for him.

We talked. Ten minutes, twenty minutes, it could have been an hour—I lost count. We talked about my trip, work, and about our children. So many things, and then again so little. He softened and hardened as we spoke, especially when I told him about Nina (in under ten words). It was hard seeing him, and good at the same time.

Then, the dreaded question. 'Were you in the neighbourhood?' he asked.

I shook my head. I told him I had been drinking coffee with a friend in Neutral Bay one minute and found myself here the next. He gave me a big hug.

When I left the store, I couldn't hold back the tears. One after the other, they ran down my cheeks. Luckily, there were only a few people out on the street because of the rain. I was soaked, and didn't care. Meeting him proved everything I knew: *why* I couldn't meet anyone else, and *what* I had been missing all that time. Nothing had changed: it was *him*, like it always had been him.

He told me of his upcoming adventure. He too would be travelling to South America very soon to celebrate his big birthday, leaving just a few weeks from now and staying for another couple.

It's hard to describe all that happened in that short period of time. It felt more like an hour that we had spoken, rather than just a few minutes. Maybe we did—all concept of time had left my mind by then.

After I left, I couldn't help wondering if he'd ever look at me the same way, knowing that it was his 'wife' that was standing in front of him. (Sadly, he never did—at least not to my knowledge.) And also wondering what had crossed *his* mind all the while we talked.

Reflections and new beliefs

I might have found my new favourite place in the city! It came in the form of a little coffee shop in Paddington, with books stacked all over across three floors. *Heaven*!

Dangling above my head was a lamp from the sixties, while the guy to my right was mixing music on a device that looked like it had just jumped out of the latest *Back to the Future* movie. His name was Magnus, an avid photographer who wrote music while working for a marketing firm. He had moved to Sydney from Sweden a few years back, I would later find out. He also happened to *really* like birds, I observed, when one flew in and stole half of his croissant from the table. He shared what was left of the croissant with said bird later, much to the dismay of the owner of the place.

There was an array of books wherever you looked, stacked neatly between velvet chairs and chandeliers, and big stony walls shimmering under the dimmed lighting. I looked at the books and their titles, wondering about the people who wrote them, the challenges they faced and the aches they turned into craft. It made me remember what inspired my first two books, and I wondered if they had felt the same—and if I would find their life stories within those pages as well, rather than the product of 'just another creative outlet'. Those were the books I was usually most interested in—especially if they came in the form of a romance.

So, after a very fulfilling morning and afternoon at the coffee shop, I came home and watched *Doom of Love* that night. No, I hadn't suddenly lost my optimism: despite its title, this movie told the story of a couple who found love following a financial breakdown, with an emphasis on self-love/self-worth and presence over possessions.

There were two things that stood out to me in that movie:

1 How lost one of the characters was, who was all about chasing money. His dream was to sit at the best table in a restaurant, and to get there he took pretty much any job he could get, growing more and more miserable by the day. I had been fortunate enough to have dined at the best tables as part of my previous role, and knew that they were not the answer. As the movie continued, part of me wanted to tell him so badly that this was not where his happiness was. Luckily, he got there in the end.

2 To challenge the requirement of effort. The female lead in the movie, who was in love with the guy chasing money, made a point about how our goals enslaved us.

Now, that one took a moment to get on board with. After all, vision plans and goal maps had been part of my yearly planning process for over a decade, and played a huge role in my success. Her point was, though, that it was those same goals that made us work for them all our lives, until we finally achieved them and realised that they weren't what we thought they would be.

She had a point there, at least based on my experience working in the corporate world. But that wasn't why that statement made me think: rather, it was her emphasis on the journey over the goal, and about enjoying the moment so much that it didn't get lost by the time we reached our destination.

I thought about it in the context of my current situation—with work, with Jimmy, and to some degree with my family. I hadn't looked at the journey lately, but purely at the hard facts lying in front of me. Quitting my job had:

- inspired me to write more than I ever had, and was the catalyst for me to submit not one, but three books to a publishing company;

- made me explore a new business opportunity with Julia, and the wellness business overall;

- convinced me to sign up to give a TED Talk; and,

- helped me address things with my family that had been on my mind ever since I was little.

Inside the whirlwind, it didn't feel so great—in fact, it felt scary and nearly impossible at times. But now that I had some distance, all of that had fallen off. Nina had fallen off, and with that, all my anger towards her. Everything that had to be said had been said. I wasn't afraid of her any more, nor did I come at her from a place of anger and hurt.

The same applied for Emily, my neighbour's ex-girlfriend. I took a very different approach in my responses to her now, compared to just a few months back.

With all of that in mind, I shot a message off to Jimmy:

'Was great to see you yesterday... Catch-up properly some time?'

Wish me luck!

Soul talk

I deleted my Instagram account from my phone that same evening. Ever since my phone broke, it was the only way I could get hold of Jimmy, and I knew that if I didn't get rid of it, I'd be staring at my phone every few seconds, waiting for his reply. Sometimes, these things were simply good measures of self-care, like leaving your phone behind to go on a hike. (*Crazy idea, I know!*)

So, instead of doing what I would normally do—re-reading my messages a thousand times, personalising it and questioning *everything* I said (and why!)—today, I gave myself a pep talk.

I told myself how proud I was of myself for following my heart, and that there was *nothing* I could do wrong when a person was meant for me. That, even if it went nowhere from here, it wouldn't be because I had done something wrong—it would just mean that I wasn't his girl. It would hurt, sure, but it wouldn't be the end of me—I would simply continue my journey alone. I stopped myself at that last part, and changed it to: *continue my journey with friends by my side, and people who genuinely cared for me.*

I then reminded myself of just how many people lately had thought I was interesting, funny, warm and kind—including Magnus, who had expressed that to me just the other day. Yes, none of them were who I wanted to be with romantically right now, but it showed me that I hadn't lost my touch. That I was still as worthy as ever.

I then treated myself to some flowers, and gave myself all the love I usually gave to others, especially on wet and cloudy days like these.

Speaking up!

I heard back from my company last night, and it wasn't good news: my request for financial compensation had been declined. (In hindsight, a pretty ridiculous request.)

When it came to my exit interview, I didn't hold back. I told our HR representative how disappointing that decision was to me, after I had worked for the company for over a decade, and how it left a very sour taste in my mouth considering how hard I always fought for our people and business. For the rest of the call, I focused on everything that was working in the office, and opportunities for improvement for the rest of the group.

On the personal front, that same week I introduced my son to an old Russian movie—a movie full of messages about how differently our lives can play out depending on the decisions we make. It was a movie that had always stood out to me, ever since I was a kid.

It brought up great conversations between us, until we were interrupted by a call. During this call, his dad somewhat flippantly dismissed the movie and it's worth.

It gave an opportunity for us to align on values. Mine differed slightly from his, and that was okay. What wasn't okay was to have this conversation in front of our son, which I communicated politely. And while we disagreed on this topic, he did circle back with some suggestions of other movies he thought were more child appropriate later that night.

Meanwhile, I got a notification: Jimmy had opened my text.

What a ride!

I did it!!! I pitched my technology idea to the virtual reality start-up this morning. I was *so* nervous before we started the call, even though I had no coffee *and* a quick yoga session just before we met. But it went as well as it could have, and ended with an agreement to talk further in another meeting, as well as several message exchanges back and forth.

The conversation challenged me to put into practice what I was trying to get out of the collaboration. I was honest: I told the founder of the company what I knew I needed from her and everything I was willing to give in return, as well as my preparation up until that moment. It felt authentic and promising when we hung up the phone.

Later that day, I had the most heart-warming exchange with my sister. We finally talked, three weeks after our last conversation, and the time between seemed to have done wonders for both of us. This time, we were able to truly hear each other, and see the challenges and opportunities in both of our lives. I hung up the phone about forty minutes later, feeling very content.

Following that talk with my sister, I called my boss to finalise my replacement.

Somewhere in between, I found a message from Jimmy, who agreed to get together after the school holidays. *Great!* Except it wasn't. Something had shifted inside me—even though I couldn't yet explain what it was.

That feeling was confirmed all the more that night, when (in my dream) several Disney princesses walked off from their princes, halfway through their kiss.

What did all of that mean?

I UNDERSTOOD as soon as the following day: I had let go of the fantasy and the dependency, or the *need* for having a partner in my life. It didn't change how I felt about Jimmy, of course—apart from the anger bubbling inside my chest, which didn't make sense until I realised its origin.

I had always put my partners on pedestals, believing *they* were perfect, and myself not so much. After all, as every Disney story taught us growing up, the female was the one who needed saving. So surely, something had to be wrong with *her*, right?

My anger faded after I wrote all of that out, but I had no intention of replying, and that persisted even as the day progressed. Now *that* was unusual for me: I normally replied to messages very quickly, in relationships more than anything. *What was stopping me?*

Dan's message popped into my head. His intuition had told him that my needs needed to be celebrated, without my having to fight for it. He proposed a grand gesture to do just that.

I thought about how desperately I wanted to see Jimmy just a few days back. *Where did that all go?*

Wherever it went, I decided to wait until it felt right, and until then to listen to whatever was stopping me from responding.

I ENDED up replying just before bed, telling him I would be away the weekend after the holidays while clarifying what day he was leaving for Peru. His reply came only a minute later—something he had never done before—asking me where I was going. Unfortunately for both of us, I didn't see that message until the next day.

When I replied, I told him where I was going, and asked him who he was travelling with, in return. *No more holding back.*

The rollercoasters I was going through with him are hard to explain, but whatever had shifted had done so decisively. It was then I realised something had changed. No longer did I put him on a pedestal.

We still exchanged about Peru and that was that. So the moral of this story is: treat the medicine with care and love yourself more than anything. While it can heal you from the past, it won't avoid mistakes going forward. That one is on you—or me, in that case.

I then realised that all that had to go into this book was already inside the book, and that—as I was nearing the end of this chapter—all the lessons were coming to an end.

Over the past six months, I had addressed boundaries outside the family, within the family, with my son, my workplace, my neighbour and my friends. All that was left was to figure out where I stood in my relationship.

So, what are my reflections from this book? Setting boundaries doesn't come easy, but it needs to be done.

I have found it most liberating to go on this journey. And while I regretted it at times, I am proud of the person I am becoming. As a result of it.

So, join me on my next path, as I launch my own business and kick some more ass! Meanwhile, don't be afraid to be who you are and speak what you must. You won't believe how liberating it feels to finally break free!

With all my love,

Tatjana Genys

www.ingramcontent.com/pod-product-compliance
Lightning Source LLC
Chambersburg PA
CBHW021637120626
46545CB00002B/589